# Country & Blues Guitar for the Musically Hopeless

*A book plus two cassettes
musical multi-media
package by
∾ Carol McComb ∾*

**KLUTZ PRESS · PALO ALTO, CALIFORNIA**

Illustrations © 1986 by Barry Geller

Published by Klutz Press, Palo Alto, California

ADDITIONAL COPIES
Individual copies of this book, as well as a current
catalog of all the Klutz titles, are available directly
from the publisher. See back pages for details.

ISBN 0-932592-12-0

9 8 7 6 5 4 3 2 1

# The guitar wasn't my first musical victim.

*When I was about 6 or 7 my family kept an old piano out in the garage. Thinking it needed some sprucing up, my brother and I saved up our allowances and bought the necessary supplies for a brand new black and white paint job.*

*As we carefully re-painted the keys, we failed to notice a general sticking together problem—until our mother came home. After a very long silence her only words were, "When you grow up, and you don't know how to play the piano, THIS is why."*

Carol McComb

# Contents

## Introduction
How to Use This Book
How to Use These Tapes
Stringing
Tuning with the Tape
Tuning without the Tape

## The REAL Beginning

## The Next Level

## Appendices

# Tape Contents

**Section 4**  *Stewball Mit Bass Runs*
Brush-Ups
*Swing Low, Sweet Chariot* with Brush-Ups
*Get Along Little Dogies*
Hammering On
*Yellow Submarine* with Hammer Ons
The Bm Chord
*Help!*

## Side Four
*Old Blue*
*Michael Row the Boat Ashore*
*Single Girl*
*Red River Valley*
*Streets of Laredo*
*I Ride an Old Paint*
*Columbus Stockade*
*This Little Light of Mine*
*Stewball*
*Down in the Valley*
*My Home's Across the Blue Ridge Mountains*
*Kumbaya*
*Woke Up This Morning*
     *with My Mind Stayed on Freedom*
*Shady Grove*
*Scarborough Faire*
*St. James Infirmary*
*Swing Low, Sweet Chariot*
*Wabash Cannonball*
*Wayfaring Stranger*
*Good Shepherd*
*One Morning in May*
*Circle 'Round the Sun*
*Bye Bye Love*
*Get Along Little Dogies*
*Help!*

# Introduction

*I* WAS 13 WHEN I PICKED UP MY FIRST GUITAR.

It was love at first sound.

My family remembers that period a little differently but they weren't listening with my ears. I thought it sounded wonderful. A little muffled maybe, a few sour notes, but I figured it's the thought that matters. And the spirit. At the time I was surrounded by the beginnings of the folk music revival. And I was determined not to be left behind. Just by picking up my new guitar and abusing a couple of chords, I was a genuine, teenage, slightly timid part of a nationwide movement. Me and Bobby Dylan.

The honeymoon lasted most of that year and part of the next. I had a handful of my very own unique chords and a dog-eared copy of a Burl Ives songbook which I played over . . . and over . . . again.

What had long since become clear to the rest of my family finally became clear to me.

My needle was stuck. I was trapped in the Endless Beginner Syndrome. Like most people I'd figured that once you picked up the basics, some kind of ball would start rolling. Pieces would fall into place. New songs and techniques would eagerly teach themselves to you.

It's a cruel myth, of course. It wasn't until I actually tracked down some real live guitarists and watched and listened did I finally begin to get myself untracked. Music, I discovered, may be a very personal form of expression, but it's also a very communal language, a Planetary Potluck with everyone milling around, adding and taking liberally from a common table.

This book and set of cassettes is your invitation. Whether you're unsure about which end of a guitar to pick up, or whether you've learned a couple of chords somewhere along the way but found yourself stuck in an early-going rut, I've tried to put together a package that can help. You don't need to be able to read music, or understand a thing about theory, it'll only slow you down. I'm an anti-instructions music instructor ("If it's not fun, it's not music"), and that means a heavy reliance on singing and songs, and a real light once-over on the "minor seventh, flat nine, augmented 5th" sort of thing.

But what about raw, native, God-given ability? What about the fact that you can't hold a tune in a large bucket? What about your ears of tin and throat of gravel?

Actually I've got a theory about that . . .

## Talent, Schmalent

I've been teaching guitar for years. I've had thousands of students. Many of them—most of them—thought they were every bit as bad as you think you are. What's more, they had proof: ("My music teacher retired after my first lesson" . . . "I used to sing in the shower. My parents soundproofed the door" . . . etc.). Self-described Musical Marginals.

But they weren't and you're not.

Musical ability is standard human equipment. It's not an option; you're stuck with it. You can't talk understandably without tone and pitch control. You couldn't distinguish the Rolling Stones from Lawrence Welk if you were really tone-deaf and if you think you're rhythm-free, just turn on the record player and watch your foot.

The question isn't "Are you musically talented?" but really "What are you going to do with all this newfound talent of yours?"

## Music Is Not a Spectator Sport

Music is communication—probably a higher form—and if you enjoy listening to it, you're only in on half the fun. So don't waste time worrying whether you've got Mozart's ear or Caruso's voice, just plug in your tape and turn the page and I'll tell you how to tune your guitar, raise your voice and join the choir.

## How to Use This Book

This book is only half of a multi-media presentation. The other half is audio: Two 75-minute cassettes that are programmed to accompany the text. Music being what it is, you really need both book and tape to make the best sense of all this, and I would go to some lengths to secure a cassette tape player. Any kind will do.

Once that's accomplished, probably the most practical way to approach this package is to (a) read all the introductory material up to page 17 of the book, skim through the rest in 10 minutes or so just to get the basic approach and then (b) go to the tape as your primary instructor.

## How to Use These Tapes

In the tapes I'll refer you to the appropriate pages when the visual element is important or when you need to read lyrics or more information. There are 4 sections on each side of each tape. All the sections are approximately equal in length and you'll find descriptions of what's on each in the front of the book in the tape table of contents.

Note that the 4th side of the two tapes is all music. It contains complete versions of all the songs that are played in the first 3 sides. It's the place you'll go when you're tired of hearing me talk.

## How Long Will All This Take?

Everyone's favorite question. Unfortunately, the answer is always a little boring. It depends. How much time you have to practice is probably the single biggest determinant. How picky you are about your sound . . . How eager you are to learn new songs . . . How fast you can get your fingers to untangle. It all figures in.

But if I were pushed, I'd probably say two to three months, assuming you've got something approaching average hands, a couple of free hours a week, and good batteries in your cassette player. Don't worry if it takes you a lot longer than this, and don't get too excited if it takes you a lot less. The guitar is not a competitive sport.

Incidentally, when you sit down to practice, stay right next to your tape player. You're going to be using that STOP button a lot. It may be 150 minutes of lessons, but it's a *lot* more than 150 minutes of learning.

## Getting Started

Go find a guitar. Even if you don't think you have one, my experience has been that the attic and hall closet would be worth checking anyway. You'd be amazed. All you need is the basic, 6-

5

string, covered with dust model that a brother or sister of yours bought for camp 8 years ago. Check to see that it's in reasonably good shape, and that it has 6 strings or the places for them to go.

If a thorough search turns up nothing, and friends and neighbors are no help, you could be forced to go out and rent or buy one. If it comes to this, there are a couple of things to keep in mind:

(1) Remember that this is going to be your First Guitar. These are the humble beginnings you're going to be looking back on for years. (My first guitar was dug out of a friend's closet. My second was a $12 finger-killer).

The Japanese seem to make the best moderately priced guitars and I would concentrate my search in that area. Ask around and find a music store that carries at least two Japanese makes.

(2) You should be looking primarily for "feel." Tone is nice, but, at this stage, one has to be realistic. It's the fundamentals that are going to count. Is the neck too big to reach around? Are the strings too high to press down without grievous finger damage? If so, can they be lowered at the shop?

(3) The nylon or steel string question. About half of my beginning students start on nylon strings and about half on steel. Nylon is a bit easier on uncalloused fingers, but steel strings have a ring to them that nylon strings don't. If it matters to you, nearly all the professional guitarists (except classical) use steel.

Taking all things into consideration, my final recommendation is to decide for yourself. Try them both at the store, listen to the difference in sound, if you still can't work up a preference ... maybe one of them is on special?

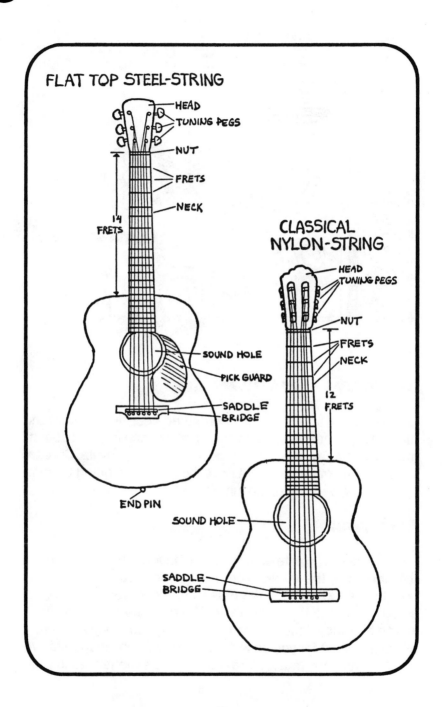

FLAT TOP STEEL-STRING

HEAD
TUNING PEGS
NUT
FRETS
NECK
14 FRETS
SOUND HOLE
PICK GUARD
SADDLE
BRIDGE
END PIN

CLASSICAL NYLON-STRING

HEAD
TUNING PEGS
NUT
FRETS
NECK
12 FRETS
SOUND HOLE
SADDLE
BRIDGE

## You've Got Your Guitar

One way or another, you've procured your first guitar. Who made it? It doesn't say, or you can't pronounce it. But it doesn't matter, someday it will be hanging in the Nashville Country Western Hall of Fame. Right now, though, we're going to try to figure out how to string and tune it.

## Stringing

This is actually quite easy. If you've bought a new guitar, have the person at the music store string it for you. If you haven't bought one, go down to the music store and buy a new set of strings. Then do the same thing. Have the person there do it. Watch how they do it, tell them you're just beginning and they'll probably tune it for you as well. If you're unlucky enough to live far away from any music store — or anyone experienced in such

8

## While You're at the Music Store

**Capos**  *elastic capo*

There's an item here that is both cheap and useful enough to justify its purchase. Called a capo (KAY-po), its purpose is to fit the sound of particular songs to the sound of your voice, if at some point you think there's a mismatch. Although there are more elaborate models available, the cheapest (and right now at least, the best for you) is the elastic variety. A couple of dollars should make you a proud owner.

*flat pick*     *finger pick*     *thumb pick*

### Picks, Finger or Flat

Picks are used on your right hand to change the sound of your guitar. They add a kind of percussive ring. A medium weight flat pick is included with this package, but you'll also need a plastic thumb pick. Which one you'll use at what time is actually a matter of individual preference, but I'll talk about that when the time comes. You may also see metal fingerpicks at the store. They're designed to slide over the ends of your index and middle fingers. My recommendation, unless you're already familiar with them, is to let these ride. Most fingerpickers (myself included) just use a thumb pick.

9

things—I sympathize. Refer to the boxed section on page 14 called "Tuning Up Without a Tape" and I'll try to lead you through it.

Incidentally, no matter who puts on your new strings, they will tend to stretch a bit before they settle in, so your sounded-great-at-the-music-store tuning job might be a little flat by the time you get home. Chances are though, unless you're already experienced in these matters, it'll sound fine to you for months, as long as nobody monkeys with the tuning pegs. If somebody does, or if your ear is especially picky, here's the procedure.

## Tuning

Tuning a guitar is one of those things much easier heard than read, so if you haven't already, pull out your cassette recorder and drop in "Side One." I'll play each string separately and your job will be to match the notes. If your string sounds too high or too low, loosen or tighten it with the appropriate peg at the top of the neck.

Sounds easy, doesn't it?

It's not.

The problem is, if you're like 99% of the human race, your ear needs to gain some experience before it can recognize specific differences in pitch. You may be able to tell that the sound on the tape is *different* from your guitar, but you won't be able to tell if it's higher or lower. It's frustrating—and *extremely* typical.

There are two time-tested approaches to this problem. I've polled my students and they seem to be evenly divided between them.

## Tuning Up With the Tape:

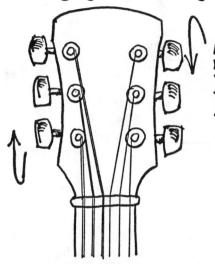

IF YOUR GUITAR IS STRUNG PROPERLY THIS IS THE WAY YOU TURN THE PEGS TO TIGHTEN THE STRINGS AND RAISE THE PITCH.

### THE DOWN AND BACK SYSTEM

**Step One:** If your string sounds "wrong" somehow, but you don't know which way, loosen it down so you know it's low (or flat, as they say). Then come creeping back up. Pluck the string, tighten a tad, listen to the correct note, then repeat. Take your time. Hum the note you hear on the tape if it helps. Console yourself with the fact that you're not playing a 106 string harp. As your guitar gets closer to the note, it gets tricky. You may not be able to tell if you've over-run the note, or if you're still coming up on it. At this point, it's time for the second step.

**Step Two:** Relax. Make your best estimate and go on to the next string. So what if you're a little off? If you couldn't hear the difference when you were tuning up, you won't hear it when you're playing either. (This is a variation on the truism that people with dull taste buds can learn how to cook very quickly.) Later on, if things start sounding a little sour, it just means your ear is getting pickier, and when you go to tune up, you'll probably be able to bring your guitar in tune a little better. In the meantime, tune up and plunge on. This is no place to get hung up.

## Tuning Up With the Tape

### THE BACK AND FORTH SYSTEM

**Step One.** Listen to the note on the tape, and if things sound a little off, but you don't know which way (high or low), flip a coin and start turning the peg one way or the other. If it starts sounding worse, reverse direction and keep going until it sounds right, or, if you over-run the note, until it starts sounding funny again. Then reverse the procedure. The idea is to try to zero in on the note by zig-zagging back and forth.

**Big Hint:** Once you've plucked the string, and are turning the peg, LISTEN HARD to the note as it changes. Just a moment or two of concentration can reduce the element of luck here quite a bit.

**Step Two.** See Step Two in Approach A.

--- **Important Postscript** ---

At the very beginning of Side One, you'll find this tuning up process in some detail, but after the first couple of times, listening to it is liable to get pretty wearisome. Consequently, at the beginning of Side Three, I've recorded an abbreviated version of the same thing for repeated use.

# And Lastly, the High-Tech Solution

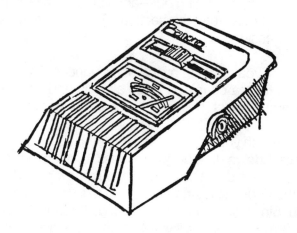

I probably wouldn't have included this a year ago, but I have recently watched these little gadgets invade my classes in swarms and I am now forced to admit that they're pretty handy.

With an electronic guitar tuner, you hit the string and a little needle tells you if you're sharp, flat or right on. It's criminally easy.

If this kind of technological bail-out interests you, trundle on down to your music store and see what they have. Or, if you don't mind waiting for the mail, we'll sell you one cheap with the order form in the back of the book.

# Tuning Without the Tape

If you're just starting out—and you have a tape player—I wouldn't even read this section. The cassette makes it that much easier.

But, if you're going by the book alone, or if you've tuned to the tape a couple of times already and are anxious to go independent, here's the procedure for tuning up solo.

Start with your lowest string (the 6th), count up 5 frets and press it down. If your guitar (bless its heart) were in tune, the pressed down sixth string would now sound the same as the unpressed string right next to it (the 5th). It doesn't? Your 5th string is out of tune. Just go through the same procedure as you would if you were listening to the correct note on the tape. Tighten or loosen the 5th string until you're happy with it.

To check the 4th string, do the same thing. Press the 5th string on the 5th fret and compare it to the open 4th. Make the necessary adjustments and go on to the next string.

Incidentally, if you don't have a guitar in your hands, reading this will make no sense at all. Actually, even with a guitar, the diagram is probably clearer. Note though that tuning the 2nd string is the exception. Check that one against the 3rd string when it is pressed on the 4th fret.

Go back to the regular technique for the last (1st) string. (In other words, press the 2nd string on the 5th fret and check the open 1st string against it.)

One more complication: The strings on your guitar are not all made the same way. Some are "wound" and some

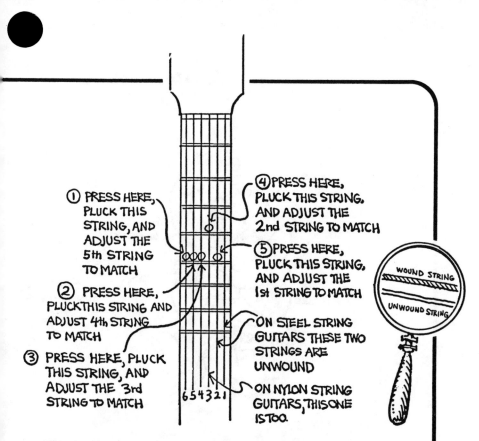

① PRESS HERE, PLUCK THIS STRING, AND ADJUST THE 5th STRING TO MATCH

② PRESS HERE, PLUCK THIS STRING AND ADJUST 4th STRING TO MATCH

③ PRESS HERE, PLUCK THIS STRING, AND ADJUST THE 3rd STRING TO MATCH

④ PRESS HERE, PLUCK THIS STRING, AND ADJUST THE 2nd STRING TO MATCH

⑤ PRESS HERE, PLUCK THIS STRING, AND ADJUST THE 1st STRING TO MATCH

ON STEEL STRING GUITARS THESE TWO STRINGS ARE UNWOUND

ON NYLON STRING GUITARS, THIS ONE IS TOO.

6 5 4 3 2 1

WOUND STRING

UNWOUND STRING

are "unwound." On steel guitars, the 1st and 2nd are unwound. On nylon string guitars, the 3rd is too. This creates a slight problem when you're checking the pitch of a wound string against an unwound string, because there's a small change in tone that can confuse your ear. (Let me define my terms: "Tone" means the quality of the sound; "pitch" means the frequency. A clarinet and a trombone can both play the same note, with the same pitch, but the tone will be quite different.) On a steel string guitar, when you're comparing the fretted 3rd string with the unfretted 2nd, you'll hear this tone difference. The trick is to ignore it and concentrate on matching the pitch. On a nylon string guitar, the problem will come up between the 4th and 3rd strings. All I can do is sympathize.

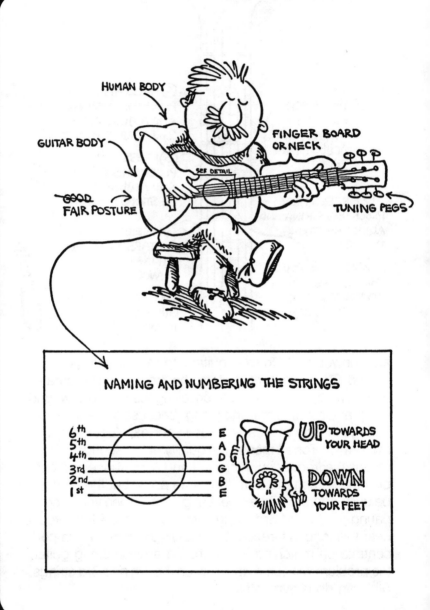

HUMAN BODY

GUITAR BODY

FINGER BOARD OR NECK

SEE DETAIL

~~GOOD~~ FAIR POSTURE

TUNING PEGS

NAMING AND NUMBERING THE STRINGS

6th — E
5th — A
4th — D
3rd — G
2nd — B
1st — E

**UP** TOWARDS YOUR HEAD

**DOWN** TOWARDS YOUR FEET

Just for future reference, here's a program to help you keep the names of the players straight. Note that the chair has no arms to get in the way, and note the guitar is held fairly snugly against your body.

The only tricky thing about all this is the way the strings are numbered. For some reason, God knows why, everybody calls the string closest to the ground the 1st string and the one closest to your chin, the 6th.

If you have trouble remembering this, just think of the most logical, sensible way to number them, then reverse it.

The strings are also named after the notes they'll sound if they're strummed open. Starting with the sixth string and working down, it goes: E, A, D, G, B, E. You can memorize this sequence with the immortal phrase: Elephants And Dogs Giggle Before Eating.

**Note for Lefties**

It *is* possible to restring a guitar in reverse enabling your left hand to do the strumming while your right hand does the fingering, but it's a hassle that's probably not worth it. Most lefties just use the conventional right-hand strum, left-hand-fingers-the-string system.

# Finally! The REAL Beginning

## Chords, A Definition

A "note" is the sound of a single string being played. A "chord" is the sound of a collection of notes played together. Roughly speaking, the notes are the letters and the chords are the words of your musical vocabulary. Learning how to form chords by fingering the right strings on the right frets is what guitar playing, and this book, are all about.

Despite the fact that there is literally a lifetime's worth of chord possibilities up and down the neck of your guitar, the vast majority of popular and folk music is built upon an embarrassingly small number of basic chords. Entire rock and roll empires have been built on little more than half-a-dozen chords and a set of drums.

So what are you waiting for?

## Your First Chord: A

Chords are identified by the first 7 letters of the alphabet, and the first one you're going to be learning is (appropriately enough) the A chord. It's the one I started with too — maybe because it's such an easy one to picture. The drawing will give you the idea of where to put your fingers and the tape (Side One, Section One) will give you an idea of how it's supposed to sound.

Incidentally, which fingers you use is not really that important, although I would recommend that you use one finger per string.

Since this is going to be your very first time playing a chord, I'm going to talk about the experience in something dangerously approaching tedious detail. Try to bear with me.

# THE THREE WAYS TO FINGER AN A CHORD

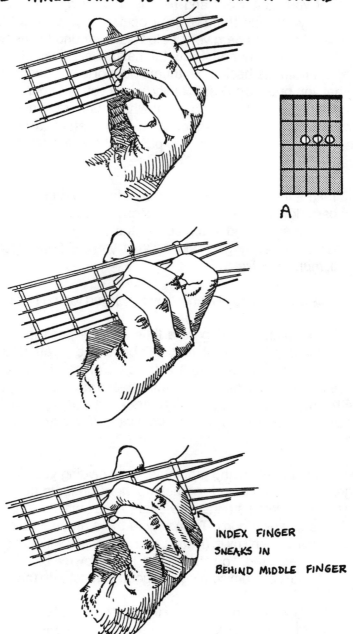

A

INDEX FINGER
SNEAKS IN
BEHIND MIDDLE FINGER

Get your guitar out and hold it on your right leg, snug up against your body. If you've got it located right, you wont' be able to see the fingerboard very well. Reach around the neck of the guitar with the fingers of your left hand, leaving your thumb still visible from the back. Your thumb supports all your chords. It's what you press *against* actually, when you put your fingers on the strings. It should go somewhere underneath the chord you're forming. Where exactly is a matter of hand size and personal preference. The picture shows a pretty typical arrangement.

Take a look again at the A chord diagram and try to fit your fingers down in their proper places. It'll seem crowded. Now with your right hand strum across the strings. On the tape this creates a clear, ringing chord. What you will hear though is a dull, muffled noise.

This is the sound of a chord being played for the first time.

Try arching your fingers a little so they don't lean against neighboring strings that shouldn't be fretted ("fretted" incidentally, just means "fingered"). In the case of the A chord, check to see that the 1st string (the one farthest away from you) and the 4th string (third from your chin) are really "open," or unfretted. You can do that just by hitting them individually and listening for any muffling.

If you're still having problems, try crowding your fingers together even more and scrunching them closer to the fret. Play each of the three strings individually to see which strings sound clear and which don't. Then wiggle them around a bit more to see if that doesn't fix it. (*Note:* Long fingernails will be a problem on your left hand. You should trim them down a bit if they keep your fingertips from coming into good contact with the strings.)

With any luck, you'll be able to hold this chord down for short, awkward little stretches good for two or three strums or until the

20

finger pain gets to be a problem. This is the Standard Beginner Experience that everyone goes through. Take heart, though, it never gets any harder. My advice is to relax. You're started on the right path. Your fingers will get tougher, stronger and more flexible soon enough. In the meantime take frequent little "my-fingers-are-killing-me" breaks and sing loud. Which reminds me. Time for your first song.

## OLD BLUE
(each slash represents one strum of "A")

/ / / /    /    /  / /
Had a dog and his name was Blue
/ / / /    /    /  / /
Had a dog and his name was Blue
/ / / /    /    /  / /
Had a dog and his name was Blue
/  /  /  /    /  /  / /
Betcha five dollars he's a good one too.
// / // / /   /  // /
Here Blue,  you good dog you.

This song actually sings a whole lot better than it reads, so I would get the tape player out and plug in Side One, Section Two where you can hear the melody and rhythm. Then play and sing along. Muffled A chord and all, you'll sound great.

# Flat Picks and Thumb Picks

Picks are used to give a little more volume to your guitar playing. They add a percussive sound.

On the tape I'm mostly using a thumb-pick. If you like the sound, put one on and see what you think. If it gives you a lot of problems, you might just skip it—at least for now. At the beginning, it seems a shame to compound your difficulties when just coordinating your left hand is such a full time job.

Alternatively, you can try holding the flat pick— although it also takes a bit of getting used to. There's an uncomfortable tendency to hold it white-knuckles tight. Hold it too loose though and you'll find it flying around the room. In addition, you have to teach your brain and hand where the end of the pick is, so that you can find the strings with it.

I suspect that you'll eventually want to know how to use both these styles, and if you're one of those responsible people who like to plan ahead, then maybe you should make the effort to learn now. Or, if you're not, you can take the short-term immediate gratification route and use your fingers unadorned.

# On the Subject of Singing

First of all, you're wrong. You can sing.

And I'll prove it.

Try phrasing the sentence "I'm an incredible singer," first as a statement, then as a question. If you can manage that — if you can lower your voice to make it a statement or raise it at the end to indicate a question — then you're onto the primary skill in singing. Pitch control. Fine tuning this control, learning how to raise and lower your voice by specific increments, is the heart of singing. It's a skill. And like any other, you get better with practice.

With the possible exception of the lady on the phone who tells you the time, nobody is a hopeless singer. Humans are born to it. Whether your voice is Joan Baez silk or Johnny Cash gravel is beside the point. That's the quality of your sound. Part of the whole unique I-gotta-be-me package of yours. Maybe it's not an operatic tenor, but a lot of people can't stand the opera. Open up and give the world a chance to hear you. Maybe you'll grow on them.

"But what about range?" you're saying. You're bullfrog low or Tinkerbell high, and it sounds a little funny or strained when you're singing along with these chords.

First of all, congratulations. The mere fact that you can even tell that kind of thing means you've got an ear with some experience. Most beginners sing and play right along with anyone from the Vienna Boys Choir to the Volga boatmen without a care in the world. And that's fine. The world's a better place every time another voice is raised in song. Even if it is a little off-key.

It may not happen right from the beginning, but people with voices pitched significantly higher or lower than mine may eventually start to notice that things are sounding ... a little funny. They're either not singing with the guitar chords, not singing with me, straining to hit notes ... or something.

## The Capo Solution

No problem. Just pull out that capo that you were supposed to buy at the beginning of this book. The $2.00 elastic variety. Strap it on the guitar neck like the illustration and pick a fret to put it on. This is trial and error time. Play and sing along with the tape on a song that's been a strain for you. Sing in your normal comfortable voice and move the capo around from fret to fret until the guitar sounds "right." Finger the chords in exactly the same way as before. What you're doing is moving the music around to fit your voice.

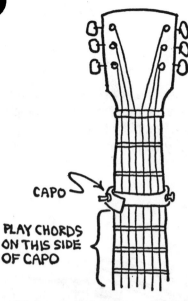

CAPO

PLAY CHORDS
ON THIS SIDE
OF CAPO

You SHOULD USE A CAPO
ONLY IF YOU THINK ONE SONG
OR ANOTHER IS TOO HARD
FOR YOUR VOICE TO REACH.
YOU MAY NEED IT FOR A FEW
SONGS, FOR NO SONGS, OR
FOR LOTS OF SONGS.
WHERE YOU PUT IT, OR EVEN
IF YOU USE IT, DEPENDS ON
THE SONG AND YOUR
INDIVIDUAL VOICE.

Listen for what sounds "right," and leave the capo there for that song. If it *all* sounds OK to you, no matter where the capo is, that's great. Just take the capo off and let's get back to our lesson. If my range and yours really are different, you'll pick up on that at some point when your ear gains a bit more experience. Then you can go back and try this capo trick again. But in the meantime, remember there's only one test that matters—does it sound all right *to you?*

And if you're not sure, give yourself the benefit of the doubt. (We're easy graders around here.)

*Postscript:* If all this leaves you a bit confused, remember it's on the tape as well.

## Your Next Chord: The E

It's not really necessary to master the A chord before you tackle this next one. Right now, one of the most important things you're learning is finger strength and flexibility (and callousing), and all the chords teach that equally well, particularly here at the beginning.

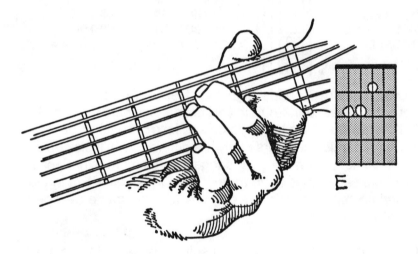

E

If you've gone through *Old Blue* a couple of times, and can stumble onto a clear ringing A chord every once in a while, I'd say that's good enough. The E chord is actually needed for a proper rendition of *Old Blue* and besides, it has a beautiful, deep ring to it.

Put the index finger (the one you point with) of your left hand on the third string (from the ground!). Locate it just behind the 1st fret. Your middle finger goes on the 5th string, and your ring finger on the 4th string. Put them both just behind the 2nd fret.

Your thumb should go underneath the second fret and you can use either just the tip of it, or, more comfortably probably, the whole thing, like the illustration. Locating your thumb like this creates something that I call "the cradle position," and I've found it to be more comfortable than just using the tip. Unfortunately, some chords (for example, the "A") aren't usually reachable from the cradle position because it doesn't allow the fingers to arch high enough—making the first string sound more like a blip than a note. When that happens, press with less of your thumb, even though it makes everything seem even more awkward. Bear with it as best you can. It'll eventually get easier. Trust me.

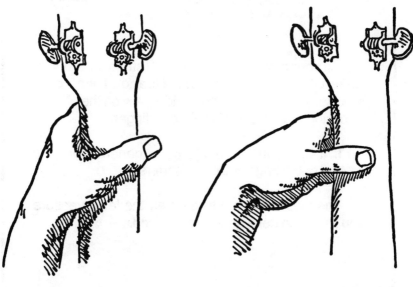

CRADLE POSITION                    NON-CRADLE POSITION

# Troubleshooting a Buzzy or Muffled Chord

• If your chord buzzes, check to see that your fingers are scrunched up close to the fret and that you're pressing hard enough. Clip your fingernails if they're keeping you from making good contact.

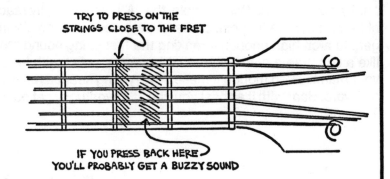

TRY TO PRESS ON THE STRINGS CLOSE TO THE FRET

IF YOU PRESS BACK HERE YOU'LL PROBABLY GET A BUZZY SOUND

• If it sounds muffled, pluck each string individually to see which are clear and which are not. Then look to see that you're not leaning accidentally on the offending string(s) with one of your other fingers.

• If it still sounds funny, try a general wiggling around of the fingers. Does wonders.

• The closer you are to the fret, the less pressure you'll need to get a good, clear sound.

Once you've got your fingers in place (you think), try strumming across all six strings with your right hand. Chances are you'll hear the familiar buzzing, muffled sound of a first-time chord. Go through the same procedures you did before with the muffled A chord. Check the illustration to make sure your fingers are located properly. Wiggle them around, press a little more firmly, scrunch them up a little closer to the fret. Then try again and use the tape (Side One, Section Two) to hear how it sounds when I play it.

## How to Imprint a New Chord

Cleaning up the sound of a chord is basically a function of building up your strength while paying attention to the hints about finger placement that I've already outlined. The principles are the same for every chord, and I promise not to drag you through the same lecture every time I introduce a new one. Let's just both assume that there'll be a break-in period for each chord during which time it will seem totally impossible, but that the tricks that worked before to get rid of all the buzzing and muffling on the old chords will eventually work again on the new ones.

Memorizing a new chord, though, is a second kind of problem. You have to teach the muscles and nerves of your hand to instinctively drop into a particular position every time the song comes around to that chord. Mostly this is just a question of time and familiarity, but there are a few secrets that can hasten the process.

Before you try to incorporate a new chord into a song, take it aside and kind of examine it. Look for anything that makes it feel, look or sound different. In the case of the E, think about how it feels to have the index finger up and away from the other two. Form an image of the chord and try to store it away in the memory banks. You're meeting strangers here and if you want to remember their faces and names later you're going to have to take a good hard look at them right now.

## Your Next Song

Enough talking. Back to the music.

**YELLOW SUBMARINE WITH SLASHES**
(Side One, Section Two. Again, one strum per slash.)

**A** / / / **E** / // / / // **A** / //
*We all live in a yellow submarine, yellow submarine, yellow submarine,*
**A** / / / **E** / // / / // **A** / //
*We all live in a yellow submarine, yellow submarine, yellow submarine.*

I'm not positive there's an advantage to putting all these slashes here, but you can always get the same idea from listening to the tape.

## Backtracking for a Minute

Now that you're starting to fumble around with the E chord, we can go back and do a proper job on *Old Blue* which actually needs the "E" as well as the "A." Here are the lyrics again with the real chord changes noted.

## NEW IMPROVED OLD BLUE

**A** / / /     /    /   / /
*Had a dog and his name was Blue*
**A** / / /     **E**    / **A**   /
*Had a dog and his name was Blue*
**A** / / /      /    / / /
*Had a dog and his name was Blue*
   /   /    /     **E**   / **A** /
*Betcha five dollars he's a good one too.*
**A** / // /   / **E**    / **A** / / /
*Here Blue, you good dog you.*

Listen to the tape (Side One, Section Two) for the beat and melody again. Note that you stay on the E chord for only two strums.

This means that you'll not only have to get your fingers off the "A," reformulate them all and then get them down on the "E," but you'll have to do this quickly. And then do it again one line later. Meanwhile you're supposed to be staying on the beat and remembering the words.

Tricky, isn't it?

Actually, at this stage in your career, it's probably too tricky. If it is, let me recommend a couple of things.

31

First, turn off the tape and practice the "A" to "E" chord change all by itself for a moment. You might know the two chords by themselves tolerably well, but you still have to learn how to get from one to the other—and back. Then go back to the slowed down version on the tape and play along while you're just humming. Forget the words for now. Concentrate on staying on the beat and keeping your fingers from tangling up in the changeovers. For right now, that should be plenty. Do this for a minute more, then take a break. Go bake some brownies.

## Back again

As an exercise, put your fingers down on an "E" and then take them off and wiggle them around. Now try to replace them. What happened? Did your fingers all go back to the right strings and frets for an E chord? (Am I kidding?) So rearrange them correctly, stare at them again and think about where they are. Then do it again. This may seem like a tedious exercise (actually, it is a tedious exercise), but you'll find that if you take a few minutes every time you're introduced to a new chord for this "fingers down on the chord, fingers off and wiggling, then down again" routine, you and your new chord will become better acquainted much more quickly.

Pop Quiz: No thinking allowed. Hit your A chord.

## Right Hand Stuff

Up to now, all your right hand has been doing is swiping at all 6 strings together. That's because getting your left hand to form chords has required the attention of more than 90% of your brain cells. This is completely typical. But it's time now to take the training wheels off. As you get a little more practiced, you'll realize that your right hand is where guitar music is really made.

For starters, we're going to separate the bottom three strings from the top three, hitting and strumming them separately, using the thumb only. As you're trying this, I'll give you a little bit of musical jargon you can sling around for effect:

—————————————— **Definition** ——————————————

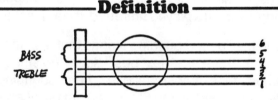

**Bass strings.** The 3 strings closest to you (#4, #5, and #6).

**Treble strings.** The 3 strings closest to the ground (#1, #2, and #3).

**And for you musical theorists** ... Strings #6–#1 are also known as E, A, D, G, B, and E because those are the notes they sound when they are strummed open (or unfretted).

—————————————————————————————————————————

The pattern we're going to be learning here is THE basic country & western, blues, folk or rock & roll guitar style.

Instead of strumming across *all* the bass strings, pick one out and pluck it separately, then finish up by strumming across all three of the treble notes. If you've got a flat pick, do it all with the pick. If not, just use your thumb.

That's it. The tape probably makes it a lot clearer, so I would switch media now to get the right rhythm and sound. But the trick is to ingrain this pattern deeply. Make it a habit.

## Which Bass Notes with Which Chords?

Every chord has a particular bass string which goes with it the best. For example, let's say you're playing your A chord. The string that sounds the best with it is the 5th string (from the ground). The 5th string, by no coincidence, also happens to be the "A" string. When it's played unfretted, it sounds the "A" note.

Along with the "best" sounding strings that accompany each of these chords, there are "next best" sounding strings as well. For the A chord, for example, while the "best" sounding string is the 5th, the "next best" is the 6th. Often times, when a song is dwelling on a particular chord, in order to create some variety in the sound, the thumb/brush pattern will alternate between these two bass strings. But it always starts on the "best" string. Your tape has it all on Side One, Section Three.

Although this sounds fairly complicated, there are really only three common bass combinations: 6th string, 4th string; 5th, 6th; or 4th, 5th. Whenever a new chord is introduced, the bass string (or pair of strings) that accompany it will be identified.

### More Right Hand Stuff

For the first few years of my guitar apprenticeship, I found myself—whether I liked it or not—playing mostly to an audience of one. It wasn't until I was about 16 that I first visited a folk music club and actually watched how the guitar was supposed to be played. Revelation!

Listening to albums, I had often heard a maze of notes being played — it sounded like separate strings being plucked — and I had wondered how they did that. Maybe they had 6 different guitarists? Each one poised over a single string?

At the time I was a complete thumb-only strummer, and I couldn't imagine how anyone could get their thumb around quickly enough to hit all those notes.

Well, as it turns out, they don't. As I discovered that evening, there are other fingers on the human hand beside the thumb, and I pass this electrifying realization along in the hopes that someone, somewhere, will be spared the three years it took me to come to it.

## Playing With More than Just Your Thumb

The following little trick will do more to spruce up your guitar playing than any other single technique in this book.

Put your fingers down on the (hopefully) familiar A chord, and leave them there for a minute.

With your right hand thumb, pluck the 5th string (remember, that's the 5th string from the ground) and then with your index finger, brush across the three strings closest to the ground, the high notes. The direction of this brush should be from the lower pitched note to the higher pitched note.

For those of you using a flat pick, all you have to do is pluck the bass note first, then use the pick to brush across the treble notes.

For those of you using a thumb pick (as I am), all you have to do is hit the bass note with your pick, then use your index finger to do the treble note brush.

This pattern of hitting first a low ("bass") note and then answering it with higher ("treble") notes is THE basic country/ western, blues, folk or rock and roll guitar style. Learn it well and you will be rewarded with an amazing amount of musical mileage. Turn on your tape (Side One, Section Three) to hear this strum.

36

# THE BASIC THUMB/BRUSH PATTERN

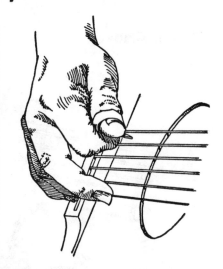

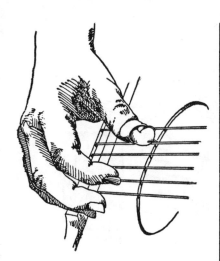

① PLUCK THE BASS

② PULL BACK INDEX FINGER

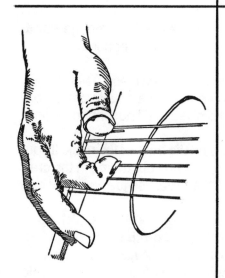

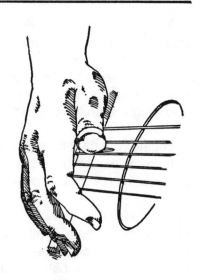

③ BRUSH ACROSS TREBLE

④ ...AND FOLLOW THROUGH

P.S. DON'T ACTUALLY THINK ABOUT ALL THESE
STEPS. JUST DO THEM.

## The D Chord

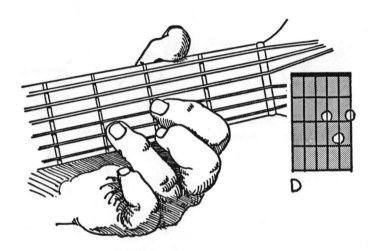

D

This was an early favorite of mine. I've always loved the way it rings. Plus, it's not too hard to finger, which never hurts.

Look at the diagram and get your fingers in place. Think about how it looks and feels for a minute and do a couple of the "off and wiggle, then down again" exercises that I described earlier.

Locate your thumb comfortably on the back of the neck. If you can do it without muffling strings, extend your thumb in the cradle position I described earlier. Otherwise, use just the tip of it.

If you strum across all six strings now, you should pick up a sour sounding note. That ought to be the 6th string (from the ground) which doesn't belong to this chord. When you strum a D, you should make a habit of skipping this string. Later on, I'll talk about why certain notes are or aren't members of specific chords. In the meantime, just follow along blindly.

For the bass/brush technique that we just covered, the bass string to hit first is the 4th. If the song dwells on the chord for longer than one bass/brush, alternate to the 5th string. Begin with the 4th, brush; then 5th, brush . . . and repeat. I realize this doesn't make any sense, but if you flip to the tape, Side One, Section Four, I think it'll start to come clearer.

## MICHAEL ROW THE BOAT ASHORE
(From now on, no more slashes. Instead, every time you see the chord, just go through the bass/brush, bass/brush pattern you just learned.)

```
A      A              A      D A
Michael row the boat ashore, Allelu-ia,
       A              E    E A
Michael row the boat ashore, Allelu--ia
```

### So You . . . Don't . . . Have . . . Any rhythm?

Before we start in on this, let's review for a moment where you are. You've been working on your two chords long enough to where you can land on them almost regularly. You've listened to the first half of Side One a couple of times and can follow along on *Old Blue* and *Yellow Submarine* reasonably well. When you pick up your guitar, people may edge away, but they're no longer leaving the house.

Congratulations. You're on your way. It's time to start thinking about your right hand and talking about putting some rhythm into your music.

Despite what you're thinking, "rhythm" (at least the way I use it) is not a technical term. Rhythm is the thing you swing your foot to—what you clap your hands by, tap your toes to, skip, dance, walk, talk and swing your kids by. The people who produced folk music (country, blues, jazz, rock and roll, bluegrass etc.) had a love for music, not a training in it. Long before anyone thought to call it 4/4 time, folk musicians were tapping their feet that way not because they'd been taught to, but because that's the way they heard it.

My understanding of rhythm came pretty much the same way—from the music. As a result, I don't *teach* rhythm so much as help you listen for it.

Which brings us back to the tape. Plug in Side One, Section Three. I'll play you a couple of strums and give you a chance to get a feel for the rhythm. Then we'll slow it down and take it together.

# A Couple of Definitions

**Musical Time.** The "pattern" in the music that you find yourself tapping your foot to. Note this is different from the "speed" of a tune. The same pattern can be played quickly, or very slowly. The "time" is the same, only the "speed" has changed. The two most universal examples of these patterns are:

**Common Time.** When a song rolls along in a pattern of 4 beats at a time (boom, chuck, chuck, chuck; boom, chuck, chuck, chuck) it's called a common (or 4/4) time tune. Most songs that come from the Western musical tradition are patterned like this. If they're not, most likely they're in . . .

**Waltz Time.** When a song's pattern is grouped 3 beats at a time (boom, chuck, chuck; boom, chuck, chuck . . .) it's called a waltz tune (or 3/4 time).

The tape has examples of both in Sections Three and Four, and I would strongly recommend you switch media now and take in the rest of this lesson via your ears.

## Some More Common Time Songs

These two songs are in common time, just like the others we've done. This just means that, for every chord you see above the words, you'll play *two* bass/brush patterns. (Confused? Try the tape).

### SINGLE GIRL

A        A      A              A
When I was single I wore clothes so fine

A        A            D         A
Now that I am married, Lord, I go ragged all the time

     E        E        A A
And I wish I was a single girl again

   E        E       A A
I wish I was a single girl again

### RED RIVER VALLEY

A         A       A        A
  From this valley they say you are going

A      A        A         E
  We will miss your bright eyes and sweet smile

E     A      A      D
  For they say you are taking the sunshine

D     E        E      A
  That has brightened our pathways awhile

A      A      A      A
  Come and sit by my side if you love me

A      A      A     E
  Do not hasten to bid me adieu

E     A      A     D
  Just remember the Red River valley

D     E      E     A
  And the cowboy who loved you so true

## From here on ...

Every time you see a chord letter written above the lyrics to a song it will represent a complete pattern of common time or waltz time.

42

## Waltz Time Tunes

Tunes in waltz time (boom, chuck, chuck; boom, chuck, chuck . . .) have a little more sway to them than common time. For example:

### STREETS OF LAREDO

<pre>
A        E         A           E
As I walked out in the streets of Laredo,
A       E      A         E
As I walked out in Laredo one day
A        E          A              E
I spied a poor cowboy a-wrapped in white linen,
A               D        E          A
A-wrapped in white linen and cold as the clay.
</pre>

Play this tune "thumb/brush/brush" to fit into its 1, 2, 3; 1, 2, 3, rhythm. The bass string pair to use for the A chord is the 5th and 6th (start on the 5th); for the E chord, the 6th and 4th (start on the 6th); and for the D chord, the 4th and 5th (start on the 4th). Alternate between these bass notes if you find yourself staying on one chord for more than one thumb/brush brush pattern. Example: On the A chord, play 5/brush/brush, then 6/brush/brush, then back to 5/brush/brush.

Here's another waltz time tune. You can hear it on your tape on Side One, Section Two.

43

## I RIDE AN OLD PAINT

D        D     D        D
*I ride an old paint, I lead an old Dan,*

A       A     D        D
*I'm goin' to Montana to throw a Hoolian*

A       A       D       D
*They feed 'em in the coolies, they water in the draw*

A       A       D       D
*Their tails are all matted, their backs are all raw*

A       A       D       D
*Ride around little dogies, ride around them slow*

A       A       D   D
*For the fiery and the snuffy are rarin' to go*

# Musical Keys

So there you are, working on your brand new D chord, trying to polish one of your three songs, when someone comes along and spoils the whole thing with the question, "What key are you in?"

No need to get upset though. There are two levels on which to answer this question. And they both give the right answer.

**(1) The Complete Ignorance Level.** You have no idea what musical "keys" are. Right now, you're still just concentrating on getting your fingers down in the right places. No problem. Just look bored and remember the following fact: Nine times out of 10, the first chord to a song has the same name as its key. *Old Paint* for example, which begins with a D chord, is in the key of "D."

**(2) The Semi-Understood Level.** The "key" is just the "stuff" from which the chords and melody of the song are made. Not only is it extremely common for the first chord of the song to be called the same as the song's key, but just about as often, the last chord is too. In addition to which, if the song is in the key of "A," the A chord is where the tunes feels "at home." If you were to stop singing and playing on some other chord, the song would sound unresolved, or unfinished somehow.

Beyond this point, the woods get very thick, and for additional information I'll have to refer you to a musical textbook where the in-depth explanations will, I think, make the Complete Ignorance Level look very attractive indeed.

## The G Chord

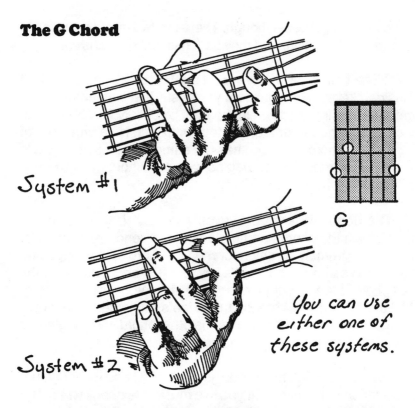

System #1

G

System #2

You can use either one of these systems.

This is a finger stretcher. Despite your first impression, it is possible. How far you can separate your fingers from one another turns out to be an adjustable physical fact. Just stick with it. Someday you'll compare your ability to spread the fingers of your left hand to your right hand and amaze yourself.

Which finger goes where is a bit up for grabs. Among the experienced, there is a preferred fingering (System #1) since it allows one to do even more impossible things later on, but at the start, most people (myself included) begin with System #2. It's easier.

Decide which of these fingerings is for you and then stay with it. Unless you want to make things even more confusing than they already are, just forget that there's any other way to do it.

46

Side Two, Section One of the tape has the following two songs and will give you a chance to fumble around with your new chord.

Incidentally, the two bass strings to use on this chord are 6 and 4 (the same as for E). Alternate them for the most interesting sound, i.e. 6/brush, 4/brush; 6/brush, 4/brush . . .

## THIS LITTLE LIGHT OF MINE

D          D  D           D
*This little light of mine, I'm gonna let it shine*
G          G  G           D
*This little light of mine, I'm gonna let it shine*
D          D  D           D
*This little light of mine, I'm gonna let it shine*
      D     A      D     G
*Every day, every day, every day, every day*
  A        D
*Gonna let my little light shine*

## DONE LAID AROUND

     G          D           D           D
*Done laid around and played around this old town too long*
D          D      G        D
*Summer's almost gone and winter's comin' on*
  D          D           D           D
*Done laid around and played around this old town too long*
  G      A     D  D
*And I feel like I've gotta travel on.*

## The Em Chord

Meet the easiest chord in this book. The "m," by the way stands for "minor," and for those curious, there's an appendix which describes the significance of the term. It's interesting from a technical point of view, but as a practical matter you can just as well skip it.

The bass strings to use are the same as for your G and E chord, the 6th and 4th (start with 6, alternate to 4).

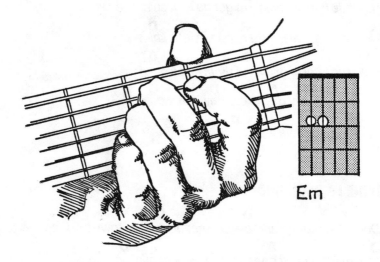

Em

Turn on your tape (Side Two, Section One) to hear Em and Stewball.

## STEWBALL

```
D    D            D    D    D    D           Em  Em
   Stewball was a good horse,   he wore a high head
Em        Em         A    A A       A        D    D
   And the mane on his foretop    was as fine as silk thread.
```

## The C Chord

Now for one of the hardest chords in this book. The C takes a full 5 fingers—everything you've got. Work on it slowly and expect some initial stress and frustration. You won't be disappointed.

The bass strings to use for the C are the 5th and the 6th (just like the A). Start with the 5th.

On the tape (Side Two, Section Two) I'll take this chord apart a bit more, finger by finger, and play a few songs that use it.

C

## DOWN IN THE VALLEY

```
C C        C C C    C      G  G
  Down in the valley,   the valley so low
G  G         G  G G  G          C    C
  Hang your head o-ver,   hear the wind blow
C  C         C   C C  C            G    G
  Hear the wind blow dear,   hear the wind blow
G  G         G  G G  G          C   C
  Hang your head o-ver,   hear the wind blow
```

As you've undoubtedly noticed by now, learning a new chord is actually only a part of the problem. Even after you've gotten it to the point where you can pull it out of thin air, or do the "off and wiggle, then down again" exercise, you still have to learn how to get to it from your other chords. You have to learn chord changes.

This is not as tough a problem as learning the chord originally, but you can still expect some fumbling around with each new song as it may present you with familiar chords, but new changes.

## MY HOME'S ACROSS THE BLUE RIDGE MOUNTAINS

```
   C      C              C   C
My home's a-cross the Blue Ridge Moun-tains
   G      G              C   C
My home's a-cross the Blue Ridge Moun-tains
   C      C              C        C
My home's a-cross the Blue Ridge Mountains, my love
   G          G         C  C
And I never expect to see you any-more
  G         G         C  C
I never expect to see you any-more
```

## KUMBAYA

```
G              G         G—C          G
 Kum - Ba - Ya, my Lord,   Kum - Ba - Ya
G              G          G          D
 Kum - Ba - Ya, my Lord,   Kum - Ba - Ya
D              G          G—C          G
 Kum - Ba - Ya, my Lord,   Kum - Ba - Ya,
G—C  G — D           G
 O Lord, Kum - Ba - Ya.
```

In this song, when I've dashed a couple of chords together, it just means play the first one for 2 beats only, then switch. In other words, when you see, G—C, it means "G, brush, C, brush."

Don't forget you're only hitting a single bass note with your thumb or pick before you brush across the treble notes of this chord. And, as you would recall if you'd done your homework, the "best" bass string for the G chord is the 6th string (otherwise known as the G note). For the C chord, it's the 5th string (the C note).

You can hear this song on Side Two, Section Three of your tapes.

## The Am Chord

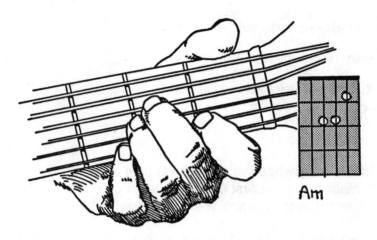

Am

An easy one. Formed just like the E chord, only shifted intact onto different strings.

The bass strings you'll be alternating are 5 and 6.

## SHADY GROVE

Am              G          Am           Am
*Cheeks as red as a blooming rose, eyes of the deepest brown*
  Am           G         G          Am
*You are the darlin' of my heart, stay till the sun goes down*
Am         G         Am        Am
*Shady Grove, my little love, Shady Grove, my dear*
Am         G         G         Am
*Shady Grove, my little love, I'm going to leave you here.*

Reading along in the book here, these new songs are coming without too much problem. Recognize though that a significant difference exists between reading them, and learning how to play them.

Sigh.

Disillusioning as this may seem, you are not going to be able to bat them out in a couple of minutes each. Don't forget, with each new song, you're actually learning: (1) A new chord (2) One or two new chord changes (3) New lyrics (4) New tempo and feel (5) New melody and (6) More finger flexibility.

Listen to the tape (Side Two, Section Three). Practice a bit, then put it down for a break. Your muscles will adapt quicker and your neurons will have a chance to digest it better. When you come back, it'll seem slightly less impossible.

## SCARBOROUGH FAIRE

Am    Am    G           Am  Am
*Are you going to Scarborough Faire*

Am    C         D        Am  Am
*Parlsey, sage, rose-mary and thyme*

  Am     C    C         G  G
*Remember me to one who lives there*

Am      G  G      Am  Am
*She once was a true love of mine*

# A Confidence Break

You've been struggling long enough. Here's a new song, with new chords, that sounds great and is easy to play. It's the way all songs would be if life were fair.

## ST. JAMES INFIRMARY

**Am7 – E7**    **Am7 – E7**    **Am7**    **Am7**    **E7**
*I went down to old Joe's barroom on the corner by the square*

    **Am7 – E7**    **Am7**
*The drinks were served as usual,*

    **Am7 – E7**    **Am7**
*And the usual crowd was there*


    **Am7 – E7**    **Am7**    **Am7**    **E7**
*Let her go, let her go, God bless her, wher-ever she may be*

    **Am7 – E7**    **Am7**
*You may search this wide world over,*

    **Am7 – E7**    **Am7**
*Never find a gamblin' fool like me*

## The Am7 Chord

Call this one the A minor 7th, and for now, don't worry about why. This is how it looks:

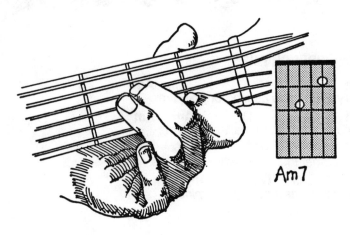

Am7

54

## The E7 Chord

This is the E7 and just as the Am7 is a variation on the Am, this is a variation on the E. You'll note (with gratitude) that your fingers are arranged in the same way for both chords, all you have to do is shift over a string to go from one chord to the next.

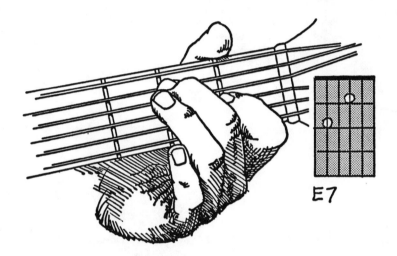

E7

You'll hear this song on the tape and I'll play it with a new strum that I'll describe to you there. Basically, it's a variation on what you already know—the *boom, chuck,* or thumb, brush thing—only this time, you'll pluck two strings, one after the other, before you brush across the rest of the chord (*boom, boom, chuck*). It's most easily done entirely with the thumb or flat pick and for variety I'd recommend that you alternate bass string pairs.

For example, on the Am7, first pluck the 5th string, then the 4th, then brush across the rest of the chord. The second time, change it a bit, hit the 6th string, the 4th string, then brush.

Using the same technique on the E7 chord translates into: 6,5, brush then 4,3 brush.

This is one of those sections that hears a whole lot better than it reads, so I'd recommend that you turn to the tape right now before this written description gets any worse (Side Two, Section Three).

## So What Have You Learned?

Up to this point, you've been working on 7 new chords, a couple of dozen chord changes, 9 songs and 3 strums. If you managed to really get those down, and happened onto the right producer, you could launch a career right now. You might not develop a reputation for instrumental pyrotechnics, but there are thousands of pop and country tunes that incorporate nothing more than what we've gone over. You'll find a half-dozen or so right in this book.

But on the other hand, there are still worlds out there to conquer. New chords, new strums, new techniques. You can consolidate what you've learned by staying on the songs that need nothing else—and you should, if only to build up your confidence and finger mobility—but you should also keep pushing. Each trick you pick up is an achievement, but it's also an appetite whetter for the next one. Which, incidentally, brings me to

## Arpeggios

You know you're finally a musician when you can throw around a little bit of Italian.

Arpeggio is a new strum technique. It simply means that each string is played individually. There's no brushing. It's a rolling sound.

Although it might seem easier at first to do this by hitting each note with your thumb or flat pick (kind a slow-motion brush) it sounds a lot better if you limit your thumb to the bass strings (4, 5, and 6) and then assign each of your other fingers one of the treble strings. For a rough idea of the motion, think of drumming your fingertips on a table top.

For a better idea, look at the illustration and listen to the tape (Side Two, Section Four). The index, middle and ring fingers should be assigned the 3rd, 2nd and 1st strings, respectively. Keeping your right hand steady and in place is obviously important here, but don't anchor your pinky finger down on the guitar (for the proper position see the illustration). For those of you who have been using a flat pick exclusively, playing arpeggios will mean using some brand new muscles, so expect some break-in problems.

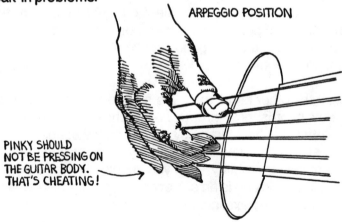

ARPEGGIO POSITION

PINKY SHOULD
NOT BE PRESSING ON
THE GUITAR BODY.
THAT'S CHEATING!

To make the arpeggio strum sound more interesting, you can alternate the bass strings, just as you've done with the thumb/brush technique.

## GYPSY ROVER

```
        D   A       D       A
The gypsy rover come over the hill,
      D           A       D A
Down through the valleys so shady
      D         A         D       G
He whistled and he sang till the green wood rang
      D       G      D G D A
And he won the heart of a la----dy
```

*CHORUS:*
```
D   A     D    A
A-ri-do-da-di-do-da-day
D   A       D   A
A-ri-do-da-di-day-di
       D                 D         G
He whistled and he sang till the green wood rang
      D       G      D G D D
And he won the heart of a la----dy
```

*Gypsy Rover* is a good song to break in this technique because the bass strings don't alternate. When you can deal with that, try this next one, where they do alternate.

## WOKE UP THIS MORNING WITH MY MIND STAYED ON FREEDOM

```
D                       D   D       D
Woke up this morning with my mind stayed on freedom
G                       G   G       D
Woke up this morning with my mind stayed on freedom
D                       D   D       D
Woke up this morning with my mind stayed on freedom
       D       A     G D
Hal-le-lu, hal-le-lu, hal-le-lu—ya
```

59

## Coming to Grips with the F Chord

F

Learning the F is basically a pain. It's arranged like the C with one additional problem—you have to cover two of the strings with only one finger. Check the illustration for the technique, but you can pretty much count on a hard time with this chord. The first string in particular will sound muffled for a disturbingly long time. All you can do is grin and bear it. If you use the chord even though it sounds bad, there will come a time, perhaps even in this lifetime, when you'll finally start to get it.

Incidentally, the bass strings to use for the F are 4 and 5 (same as the D chord). Turn on your tape (Side Two, Section Four) and practice it with me.

A good introduction for the F, *The Sloop John B* is a calypso tune that's been recorded by everyone from Harry Belafonte to the Beach Boys.

## SLOOP JOHN B

    C                    C      C           C
*We came on the Sloop John B, my grandfather and me*
 C          C       G G
*Round Nassau town we did roam*
        C  C      F  F
*Drinkin' all night, got into a fight*
       C          G         C C
*Well I feel so break-up, I want to go home.*

```
  C              C   C              C
So hoist up the John B sails, see how the mainsail sets,
C              C              G   G
Call for the captain ashore, let me go home
           C C        F      F
Let me go home,    I want to go home
   C        G         C
I feel so break-up,  I want to go home.
```

## SWING LOW, SWEET CHARIOT

```
   C              F - C  Am                G
Swing low, sweet chariot, comin' for to carry me home
        C         F - C  Am    -    G      C
Swing low, sweet chariot, comin' for to carry me home

C                         F  -  C   Am              G
I looked over yonder and what did I see, comin' for to carry me home
   C          F    -    C  Am   -   G      C
A band of angels comin' after me, comin' for to carry me home
```

## THE WABASH CANNONBALL
(located right after "Quick Tuning"
on Side Three)

```
     C          C          C          F
Out from the wide Pacific to the broad Atlantic shore
   G          G              G           G
She climbs the flowery mountain over hills and by the shore
   C              C              C              F
Although she's tall and handsome, she's known quite well by all
      G          G          G          C
She's a regular combination, the Wabash Cannonball.

C          C      C              F
Listen to the jingle, the rumble and the roar
      G          G              G          C
As she glides along the woodlands, over hills and by the shore
   C              C              C        F
She climbs the flowery mountains, hear the merry hobo squall
      G          G          G          C
As she glides along the woodland, the Wabash Cannonball.
```

## The Dm Chord

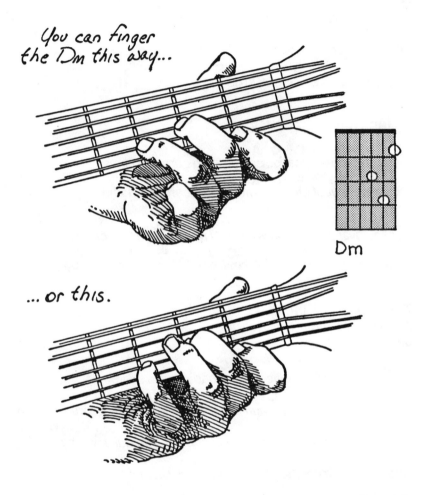

*You can finger the Dm this way...*

Dm

*... or this.*

This one's almost easy. The bass strings to use are 4 and 5 and, like the D chord, the 6 string (the one nearest to you) shouldn't be strummed. It's not a part of this chord. Note that you have a choice as to which finger to use on the 2 string. Choose one and forget about the other.

If you've been wondering what the definition of a minor chord is, but don't want to get bogged down in technicalities, this song is your answer. *The Wayfaring Stranger* has a particular sound to it, a kind of haunting wail, and it's a result of its use of minor chords.

Dm and this next song are on Side Three, Section One of your tapes.

## WAYFARING STRANGER

```
Am      Am E      Am    Am
  I am a poor, wayfaring stranger,

          Dm Dm          Am
      trav'ling through this world of woe
Am            Am E      Am    Am
  And there's no sick-ness, toil or danger,

            Dm Dm         Am
  in that bright land     to which I go
Am          F F          C    C
  I'm going there to meet my mother,

          F   F          E
  I'm going there   no more to roam
E           Am E        Am   Am
  I'm just a-go -  ing over Jordan,

          Dm Dm       Am
  I'm just a-go -  ing over home.
```

63

## The B7 Chord

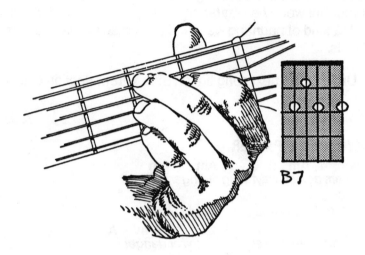

The B7 crops up every now and then, mostly in some kind of combination with the E chord. It looks bad, but actually the fingers go down in logical places for once.

The bass strings to use are 5 and 4.

### THE MIDNIGHT SPECIAL

E                               A        A                    E
  *Well you wake up in the morning,     hear the ding dong ring*
E                          B7   B7                         E
  *You go marching to the table,     see the same damn thing.*
E                A   A                E
  *Well it's on one table,     knife, fork and a pan,*
E                          B7   B7                                      E
  *And if you say a thing 'bout it,     you're in trouble with the man.*
E                    A        A        E
  *Let the Midnight Special     shine her light on me*
E                    B7     B7                            E
  *Let the Midnight Special     shine her ever lovin' light on me.*

## Moveable Chords

A few chords can be moved—fingers unchanged—up and down the neck to create entirely different chords depending on which fret you're on. (Learn one chord, get the second for free!)

The fingering for the Am, for example, can be relocated—intact—up to the 3rd or the 5th fret. Although it may not be theoretically precise, we'll just call these the Am at the 3rd fret and

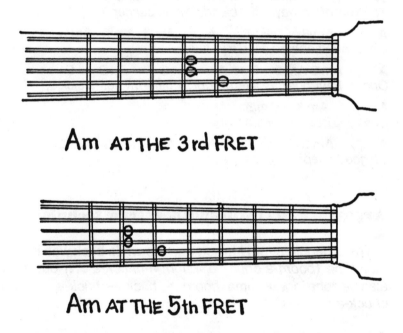

Am AT THE 3rd FRET

Am AT THE 5th FRET

the Am at the 5th fret chords (their real names come from a level of theory that reasonable people avoid).

When you play an Am in front of these two chords, you create ...

## Just About the Best Song in This Book

Go back to the *St. James Infirmary* and recall the blues strum that you learned for it. You'll use it again on *Good Shepherd* (and, as usual, you can hear it on the tape (Side Three, Section Two).

## GOOD SHEPHERD

     A  Am/3     Am/5  Am/3 A  Am/3       Am/5 Am/3
*If you want to get to heaven,        over on the other shore*

A           Am/3   Am/5        Am/3
*Keep out of the way of the blood stained banner*

A      Am/3    E     A     Am/3 Am/5  Am/3
*Oh, good Shepherd, feed my sheep.*

A     Am/3 Am/5  D   A       G          D     E
*One for Paul, one for Silas, one for to make my heart rejoice,*

A      Am/3    Am/5   D
*Can't you hear my lambs a-cryin',*

A     Am/3      E      A     Am/3 Am/5  Am/3
*Oh good Shepherd, feed my sheep.*

## Arpeggio Waltz (Still another strum technique . . .)

The arpeggio strum I talked about a while back was in common time (*boom-a-chuck-a, boom-a-chuck-a* ...) but it can also be done in waltz time (*boom-a-chuck-a-chuck-a, boom-a-chuck-a-chuck-a*).

Try drumming your fingers along in this pattern:

*Thumb-Index-Middle-Ring-Middle-Index* . . . and repeat

Note that there is no alternating bass built into this pattern, but if you stay on a chord long enough to play two patterns, it

66

DON'T FORGET.
IN THE ARPEGGIO,
YOUR FINGERS ARE
ASSIGNED SPECIFIC
STRINGS. ONLY
YOUR THUMB WANDERS
AROUND AT ALL.

sounds more interesting to alternate the bass, just as you've been doing with all the other styles.

Try *Scarborough Faire* with this arpeggio waltz. Then turn on the tape and we'll do another song that uses this same technique (Side Three, Section Two).

## ONE MORNING IN MAY

<pre>
          G        F        C          G  G
</pre>
*One morning, one morning, one morning in May*

<pre>
   G       F        C          D  D
</pre>
*I spied a fair couple a-making their way*

<pre>
   G       Em       Am         G
</pre>
*One was a maiden so bright and so fair*

<pre>
          G        C          D          G  G
</pre>
*And the other was a soldier and a brave volunteer.*

# The Next Level

### Fingerpicking the Blues

If you're this far back into the book, I suspect you're already past the point of no return, so I'm going to start introducing some more advanced things in an exploratory kind of way. The idea is to open some doors and expose you to some of the new worlds that lie beyond them.

Fingerpicking is an incredible technique that originated in the Mississippi Delta and other parts of the rural south. It probably owes its musical origins to the beginnings of ragtime piano and it manages to duplicate the same two-handed style by playing both melody and chords at the same time. And all on one guitar. Not easy, but the results are worth it.

Probably the best way to begin on this is to learn something called a "right-hand roll." This is similar to the arpeggios we've learned—just an unvarying finger pattern that your right hand has to learn.

Let's start with this one.

### THUMB — MIDDLE — THUMB — INDEX

Try drumming this on your knee for a moment. Then try it on a G chord. Use these strings:

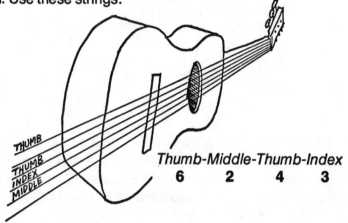

Thumb-Middle-Thumb-Index
6      2      4      3

On the C chord, use these strings:

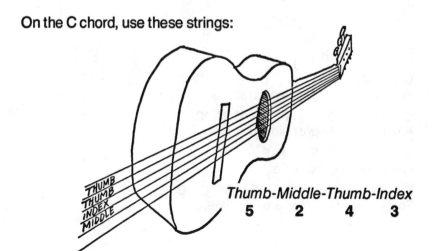

Thumb-Middle-Thumb-Index
5      2      4      3

69

On the D chord, use these strings:

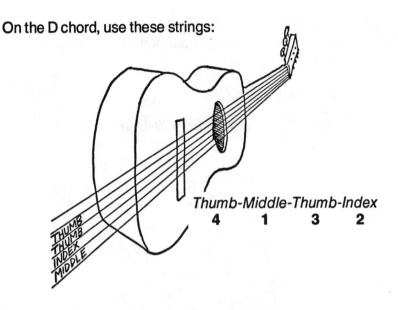

Thumb-Middle-Thumb-Index
**4    1    3    2**

Plug in the tape now (Side Three, Section Three) and I'll take you through this part slowly. *Freight Train* is the song I'll be working you towards. It was written by Elizabeth Cotten at the beginning of this century and, more than any other single tune, it has come to represent the fingerpicking style. Once you learn it, you'll become another link in an unbroken tradition. A part of the living blues.

## FREIGHT TRAIN

**C    C    C    C   G  G  G   G**
*Freight train, freight train run so fast*

**G    G    G    G   C  C C  C**
*Freight train, freight train run so fast*

**E E        E E    F F    F**
*Please don't tell what train I'm on*

**F    C    C    G    G  C  C   C   C**
*So they won't know where I've gone.*

70

## CIRCLE ROUND THE SUN

A     A  G     D     A   A  A
*I know my baby sure must love me some*

A     A  G     D     A   A  A
*I know my baby sure must love me some*

        A        A        G  D     A A
*The way you throw your arms around me like the circle around the sun*

## One Week Later

Once you've consolidated this right hand roll technique, you can begin to modify it.

Instead of: *Thumb-Middle-Thumb-Index*

You'll be playing: *Thumb—Thumb-Index*

The extra-long dash after the first "thumb" is an effort to represent the half pause you'll hear in this pattern on the tape.

All I've done is take away one of the notes you've been playing

71

in your blues roll. Listen to what this sounds like on the tape where I'll be playing around with an A chord. Practice it until it starts to feel a little familiar and then (deep breath) add your two rolls together into one long thing that looks like:

*Thumb —Thumb-Index-Thumb-Middle-Thumb-Index*

Practice this combination roll on *Freight Train* and *Circle 'Round the Sun.* Listen to the recorded versions to get the timing and feel (Side Three, Section Three).

## THE NEW IMPROVED FREIGHT TRAIN

C         C        G    G
*Freight train, freight train run so fast*
G         G        C    C
*Freight train, freight train run so fast*
E         E     F      F
*Please don't tell what train I'm on*
       C      G       C   C
*So they won't know where I've gone.*

## NEW IMPROVED CIRCLE ROUND THE SUN

A          G   –   D     A    A
*I know my baby sure must love me some*
A          G   –   D     A    A
*I know my baby sure must love me some*
       A                          G   –   D     A A
*The way you throw your arms around me like the circle around the sun*

## Bass Runs

Bass runs are another kind of embellishment to add to your playing. They can be incorporated into any of the styles we've learned so far: thumb/brush in common or waltz time, arpeggios, or fingerpicking. Side Four of the tape has examples of bass runs in all three of these styles and their variations.

As the name suggests, bass runs are played on the bass strings and are usually only a few notes long; just short bits of melody that are used to connect chords, to make your ear "expect" the next chord coming up.

Naturally, a big problem is timing. Whenever you make room for some kind of musical embellishment or filler, something from the basic pattern has to get bumped. But rather than force some kind of written explanation about this process on you (after all, how many "boom/chuck's" can you stand?) I'll just refer you to the tape where it'll be a lot easier going (Side Three, Section Three).

The song that you'll be graduating to is:

## BYE BYE LOVE

```
G  0/5  2/5 C     G   0/5  2/5 C      G
      Bye bye love,        bye bye, happiness,
    0/5  2/5 C   G       G  -  D    G
      Hello loneliness, I think I'm gonna cry
    0/5  2/5 C     G   0/5  2/5 C      G
      Bye bye love,        bye bye sweet caress.
    0/5  2/5 C   G       G  -  D    G
      Hello emptiness I feel like I could die
             G  -  D      G
      Bye bye my love-a good bye-bye
```

# The Bass Run for Any Occasion
## (as long as it's in common time)
## Chart

A word of explanation first. I'm going to resort to a bit of un-avoidable short-hand to identify individual notes so that I can get all this information onto one chart. If, for example, you should play the 5th string open (pressing on no fret) I'm going to represent that with a fraction-looking thing: 0/5. If I want you to put your finger behind the 2nd fret on the 5th string, that will look like: 2/5. The first number represents the fret, the second number represents the string. So it looks like fret/string and sounds, appropriately enough, like "frustrate."

The bass run from a G to a C is:     G, brush, 0/5     2/5,

C brush . . . and off you go.

From a C to a G:     C, brush, 2/5     0/5,     G, brush, etc.

That's the formula, here's the chart:

| From | To | Play | |
|------|-----|-----|-----|
| G | C | 0/5 | 2/5 |
| C | G | 2/5 | 0/5 |
| D | G | 0/6 | 2/6 |
| G | Em | 3/6 | 2/6 |
| Em | G | 0/6 | 2/6 |
| C | F | 0/4 | 2/4 |
| F | C | 2/4 | 0/4 |
| C | Am | 3/5 | 2/5 |
| Am | C | 0/5 | 2/5 |
| A | D | 2/5 | 4/5 |
| D | A | 4/5 | 2/5 |
| A | E | 4/6 | 2/6 |
| E | A | 2/6 | 4/6 |

# The Bass Run for Any Occasion
## (as long as it's in waltz time)
## Chart

| From | To | Play* | | |
|------|-----|------|------|------|
| C | G | 3/5 | 2/5 | 0/5 |
| G | C | 3/6 | 0/5 | 2/5 |
| A | D | 0/5 | 2/5 | 4/5 |
| D | A | 0/4 | 4/5 | 2/5 |
| A | E | 0/5 | 4/6 | 2/6 |
| E | A | 0/6 | 2/6 | 4/6 |

*When you want to include one of these bass runs in a waltz time song, the run replaces one full strum pattern (three beats).*

*Stewball* is a good song to dress up with a few bass runs. Plug in the tape to listen to *Stewball Mit Bass Runs* (Side Three, Section Four). Below are the associated visuals.

## STEWBALL MIT BASS RUNS

0/5  2/5  4/5  D        D  D  D        Em  Em  Em
*Stewball was a good horse,    he wore a fine head*

        Em        A      A A      0/5 2/5 4/5  D      D  D
*And the mane on his foretop    was as fine  as  silk thread*

75

## The Brush-Up

This is another little goodie used to fill out the rhythm. It's a right-hand technique. After you've brushed down across the strings with your index finger or flat pick (either in the common or waltz time thumb/brush pattern) you can squeeze an extra brush back up across the first string without disrupting the timing to the pattern.

The tape will give you the idea (Side Three, Section Four). I'll be re-doing a song you've already seen, *Swing Low, Sweet Chariot* (page 61) as well as a new one, *Get Along Little Dogies*.

## GET ALONG LITTLE DOGIES

G      Am      D      G
*As I was out walking one morning for pleasure*

G      Am    D    G
*I spied a cowpuncher a-riding along*

G      Am      D      G
*His hat was thrown back and his spurs were a-jingling*

G   Am      D      G   G
*As he approached he was singing this song.*

*Chorus*

     D   D    G      G
*Whoopie, ti yi yay, get along, little dogies*

     D    D      C      G
*It's your misfortune and none of my own*

     G   Am    D      G
*Whoopie, ti yi yay, get along, little dogies*

   Em      Am      D      G
*You know that Wyoming will be your new home.*

This tune is in waltz time. The brush-up gives it a kind of relaxed, rolling sound. The most common place to put it is after the second brush. This changes your pattern from thumb/brush/brush (*boom, chuck, chuck*) to thumb/brush/brush-up (*boom, chuck, chuck-a*).

## Hammering On

This is a left-hand technique, an embellishment that you've probably heard used a great deal in banjo playing. The idea is to come down on a string (with your left hand) just a fraction of a moment after it's been plucked (with your right hand). It adds a nice touch when it's used in the right places. On the tape (Side Three, Section Four) I've redone *Yellow Submarine* with hammer on's and worked a few into the completed versions of all the songs on Side Four.

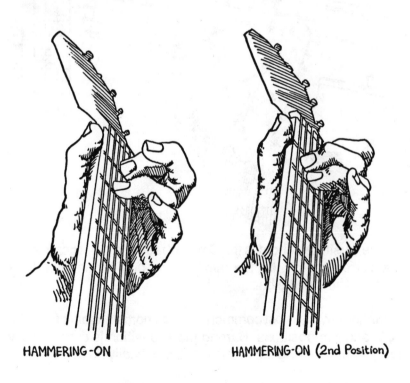

HAMMERING-ON                    HAMMERING-ON (2nd Position)

## Barring Chords, The Last Frontier

Bar chords are the last stop on your finger aerobics program. This is where it gets serious.

In the illustration here you'll see a bar across all 6 strings at the second fret. That represents your forefinger. What you'll be trying to do is clamp down all the strings at the second fret (in effect, shortening the guitar neck) and then, with your remaining fingers, forming what used to be an easy chord shape.

Try it once. You won't believe normal earthlings ever do this.

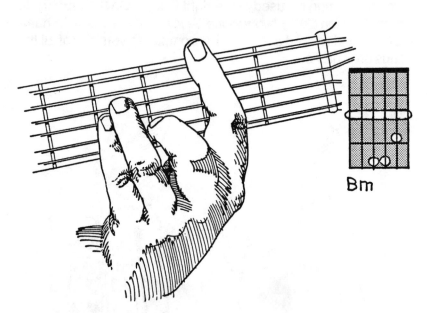

Bm

The illustrated chord is the Bm, probably the most common of the barred chords. It's the familiar Am, only formed two frets higher in front of the bar.

Generally, the most common barred chords are built from the A, E and Em positions. Barring the A position is considerably tougher and barring the D and Dm is practically ridiculous.

## What Bass Strings to Use

This is easy. Just use the bass strings you would use for the chord that has been moved up the neck. A Bm chord, for example, uses the same two bass strings as an Am, the 5th and 6th.

## Help!

Actually, that's the name of the song we'll be working towards here (it seems appropriate under the circumstances). You can hear it on Side Three, Section Four of your tapes.

## HELP!

G       G            Bm       Bm
*When I was younger, so much younger than today*

Em           Em       C - F   G
*I never needed anybody's help in any way*

G       G             Bm    Bm
*But now these days are gone and I'm not so self-assured*

Em           Em             C - F   G
*Now I find I've changed my mind, I've opened up the doors.*

Am       Am       Am Am
*Help me if you can I'm feelin' down*

     F        F        F   F
*And I do appreciate you bein' round*

D        D         D     D
*Help me get my feet back on the ground,*

      G   C       G
*Won't you please, please help me.*

"Help!"
Words and music by John Lennon and
Paul McCartney
© Blackwood Music
All rights reserved.
Used by permission.

How you end up using all the basic chords, strums, techniques and little tricks I've been describing here finally adds up to something; unconsciously, it's the way you personally express yourself through this instrument. It's your own particular musical style, and if you're this far into the instructional underbrush, I don't think it's too soon to start talking about it.

For the formerly-thought hopeless, the term "musical style" is rather imposing, but it's actually an inevitable outgrowth of learning any instrument. It's your own voice in this new language you've picked up. All the "rules" that you've learned about chord positioning and right hand techniques are just a grammar. A loose one at that. How you use, bend or even break those rules is up to you.

In the pages of this book, and on the taped instruction, there is enough musical grammar and vocabulary to enable you to sing a lot of different songs, and tell a lot of different stories. But, obviously, there's a great deal more here to be learned, some of which you'll be able to teach yourself. The Endless Beginner Syndrome can strike at almost any level though, and if you want to avoid that particular trap, as well as participate in one of life's few Truly Great Times, you'll take the next big step ...

## Finding Partners

Unlike most other instruments, the guitar is a great solo act. You can spend a lifetime combining it with your voice to create a one-person band that is uniquely flexible and multi-layered. But you'd be missing something extremely important about music if you chose that route exclusively, because nothing bonds people together the way homemade music does. Every harmonica player, every bass, banjo or guitar player, every singer, spoon clacker, drum banger, jug blower and washboard scraper is a potential part of your act—and a friend waiting to be made.

Finding other people to play with is mostly just a matter of putting yourself in the way of other musicians. Good music stores often serve as clearinghouses for people looking for musical partners, and you should check their bulletin boards, as well as those at any nearby colleges or libraries.

Keep your guitar case in full view in your living room and pull it out at the slightest provocation. You'll eventually stumble onto someone who is already plugged into a circle of musicians, and from that point on the process is easy.

And if you ever *really* want to meet more musicians, go to a bluegrass festival. You'll find people there picking 24 hours a day!

## As for me . . .

The band I spend most of my time playing with these days is a quintet. We have a banjo, bass, mandolin and a couple of guitars. Over the years though I've sat in with combinations of just about everything playable, and performed everywhere from Carnegie Hall to the Vista, California P.T.A.

But where I'm most comfortable is where there's no audience, where everyone's either playing along, or raising their voices along with mine. For me, music isn't so much a performer's art as it is the art of communication, raised to its highest pitch, and that's the best lesson I have to give you, because that's the one that can take you way past this book, and in fact, as far as you want to go.

82

# Appendices
## (Or, *a little deeper into the musical woods)*


## I. Scales

Probably the best place to conduct this discussion is on the keyboard of a piano, where the visuals are all in place.

THESE TWO KEYS ARE SEPARATED BY A "HALF STEP"

THESE TWO KEYS ARE SEPARATED BY A "WHOLE STEP"

THESE TWO KEYS ARE SEPARATED BY A "HALF STEP"

**A definition:** When two white keys are separated by a black key, their two notes differ by a "whole step."

**Another one:** When two white keys are side-by-side, with no intervening black keys, their notes differ by a "half step."

**One more:** The difference between a white key note, and the note of the black key next to it, is also a "half step."

**And finally, the big one:** A scale is a string of 8 notes, organized according to the following formula: whole step, whole step, half step, whole step, whole step, whole step, half step (two wholes, a half, three wholes, and a half).

If you randomly pick a key to start on, anywhere on the piano, and go up the keyboard according to the formula given above, you will create a scale, named after the note you started with.

If you start on the C note, creating a C scale, this is what it looks like:

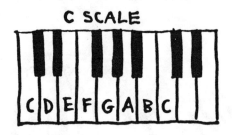

C SCALE

On the guitar fingerboard, you can raise the pitch of a string by a half step if you go up one fret; if you go up two frets, you raise its pitch by a whole step.

Using the same whole step, half step formula, here is how you would play the C scale on the guitar.

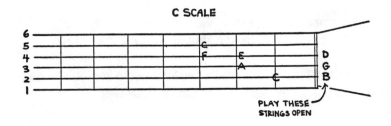

C SCALE

PLAY THESE
STRINGS OPEN

Back to the piano. Here is what a G scale would look like. You'll notice that, in order to stay in the formula, you have to use a black key between the 6th (f) and 7th (g) note. This f + 1/2 step is called an "f sharp," symbolized by f#.

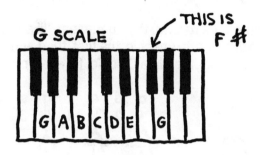

# II. Chords; Major, Minor and 7th's

Assuming you understand at least some of the previous discussion about scales, you're in a position to see how chords are usually built.

For some dark reason, the human ear "likes" particular combinations of notes, in specific, the first, third and fifth note of any scale, played together. In a C scale, for example,

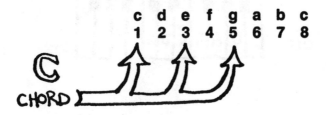

that means the c note, the e note and the g note, which together make a C major chord.

In a G scale, the 1st, 3rd and 5th notes of the scale would be g, b and d, as illustrated below. Together they make a G major chord.

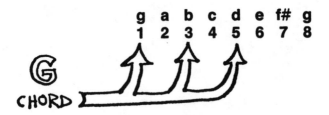

# Minor Chords

The Minor Chord Rule: If you lower the middle note of a major chord by a half step, you get a minor chord.

Example: For the C chord, the middle member is an e. Lower it a half step to an e flat and play it along with the c and the g and you'll be playing a C minor chord.

To hear this in action, play your E chord. Then lift your index finger off the 3rd string, lowering it by a half step. Welcome to the E minor chord.

Probably more meaningful though, is to listen to the difference in mood between E and Em. It's that quality that defines in practice what the above formula describes in theory.

## Minor Chord Rule of Thumb

Any song with the words "lonesome" or "woeful" in the title, or on the subjects of heartache, infidelity, train wrecks or ghosts, almost definitely makes a lot of use of minor chords.

# 7th Chords

A common variant on major chords.

Let's use as our example the G7 chord. We haven't met it before this, but you can find the fingering in the appropriate appendix.

The G major chord is formed (as described in the major chord appendix) by putting together the 1st, 3rd and 5th notes of the G scale. That translates to the g, b and d notes in the little chart below:

| (g) | a | (b) | c | (d) | e | f# | g |
|---|---|---|---|---|---|---|---|
| (1) | 2 | (3) | 4 | (5) | 6 | 7 | 8 |

Now all you need is the arbitrary, don't-ask-why rule for building 7th chords, to wit:

**The 7th's Rule:** Take the 7th note of the scale, lower it by a half step, and add that to the 1st, 3rd and 5th notes of the major chord.

In the example, the 7th note of the G scale is f#. Lowered a half step, it becomes f. So the G7 chord is a mix of the g, b, d and f.

Look at the chord diagram for G7 and play it. Then play the G. Listen for the difference in mood. Let that be your definition if all this theory makes you dizzy.

## Your Homework

*Using the formula that you've undoubtedly memorized, build a D scale and circle the three notes that together make a D chord. Use the space below and print neatly.*

**Answer:**

| (D) | E | (F#) | G | (A) | B | C# | D |
|---|---|---|---|---|---|---|---|
| (1) | 2 | (3) | 4 | (5) | 6 | 7 | 8 |

# III. Chord Fingering Diagrams

The bass and alternating bass are in parentheses above each chord.

**MAJOR CHORDS**

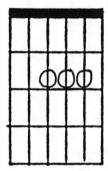
A (5,6)

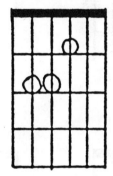
E (6,4)

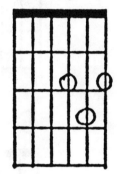
D (4,5)

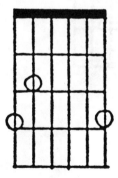
G (6,4)

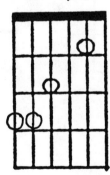
C (5,6)

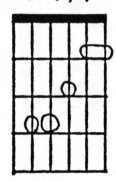
F (4,5)

## MINOR CHORDS

### Am (5,6)

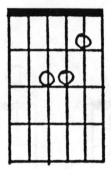

### Em (6,4 or 5)

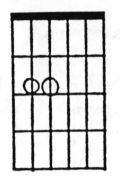

### Dm (4,5)

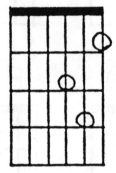

### Bm (5,6)

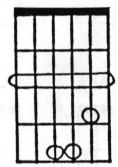

## SEVENTHS

Am 7 (5,6)

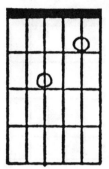

E 7 (6,4 or 5)

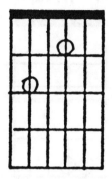

B 7 (5,4)

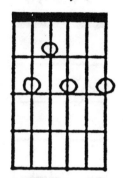

G 7 (6,4)

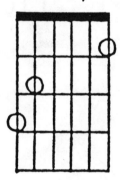

D 7 (4,5)

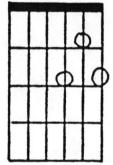

**OTHERS**

## G6 (6,4)

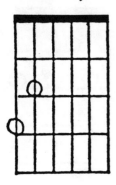

## F#m (6,4)

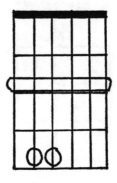

## C#m (5,6)

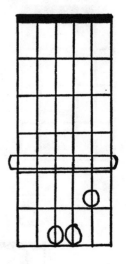

# IV. All the Lyrics to Everything You've Learned

Here are more verses to the songs we've learned. You can hear these complete versions on Side Four of your tapes, where I've added some of the fancier things like hammering on and bass runs here and there just to dress them up a bit. When I've used a capo or changed any chords for variation, I'll let you know. Also, the chords are written in only when they change. In the front of the book, they're written in every time you do a strum pattern, but I figure by now you don't need your hand held quite that tightly.

## OLD BLUE

**A**
*Had a dog and his name was Blue*
          **E**      **A**
*Had a dog and his name was Blue*

*Had a dog and his name was Blue*
               **E**    **A**
*Betcha five dollars he's a good one too.*
        **E**   **A**
*Here Blue, you good dog you.*

**A**
*Shouldered my gun and I tooted my horn*
              **E**         **A**
*Gonna find a possum in the new ground corn*

*Old Blue barked and he went to see*
          **E** **A**
*Cornered a possum up in a tree*
        **E**   **A**
*Here Blue, you good dog you.*

**A**
*Old Blue died and he died so hard*

E  A
*He shook the ground in my backyard*

*Dug his grave with a silver spade*

    E  A
*Lowered him down with a golden chain*

*Every link I did call his name*

    E  A
*Here Blue, you good dog you*

    E   A
*Here Blue, I'm a-comin' there too.*

**(pg. 21 and 31/Side One, Sect. Two)**


## MICHAEL ROW THE BOAT ASHORE

A       D A
*Michael row the boat ashore, Allelu-ia,*

   C#m  Bm  A E A
*Michael row the boat ashore, Allelu--ia*


A       D A
*Sister helped to trim the sail, Allelu-ia,*

   C#m  Bm  A E A
*Sister helped to trim the sail, Allelu--ia*


A       D A
*Jordan's river is deep and wide, Allelu-ia*

   C#m   Bm  A E A
*Milk and honey on the other side, Allelu--ia*


*Michael row. . .*

**(pg. 39/Side One, Sect. Three)**

## SINGLE GIRL
(I used a capo on the 4th fret
and played this in the key of G)

  **G**
When I was single I wore clothes so fine

                      **C**           **G**
Now that I am married, Lord, I go ragged all the time

  **D**             **G**
And I wish I was a single girl again

  **D**               **G**
I wish I was a single girl again


  **G**
Single girl, a single girl, she's goin' anywhere she please

                      **C**          **G**
Married girl, a married girl got a baby on her knees

  **D**             **G**
And I wish I was a single girl again

  **D**               **G**
I wish I was a single girl again


  **G**
Single girl, a single girl, she's goin' out dressed so fine

                      **C**          **G**
Married girl, a married girl, she wears just any kind

  **D**             **G**
And I wish I was a single girl again

  **D**               **G**
I wish I was a single girl again


  **G**
Single girl, a single girl, she goes to the store and buys

                      **C**          **G**
Married girl, a married girl, she rocks the cradle and cries

  **D**             **G**
And I wish I was a single girl again

  **D**               **G**
I wish I was a single girl again


**(pg. 42/Side One, Sect. Three)**

## RED RIVER VALLEY

(I used a flat pick on this one and
played it in the key of C. I also added
some extra chords on the choruses.)

**C**
From this valley they say you are going

                        **Am**              **G**
We will miss your bright eyes and sweet smile

          **C**                   **F**
For they say you are taking the sunshine

        **G**                       **C**
That has brightened our pathways awhile


              **C Em**  **Am G**    **C**
Come and sit by my side if you love me

               **Am**        **G**
Do not hasten to bid me adieu

          **C**                 **F**
Just remember the red river valley

        **G**                  **C**
And the cowboy who loved you so true


          **C**        **G**        **C**
Do you think of the valley you're leaving

              **Am**      **G**
O how lonely and sad it will be

          **C**                  **F**
Do you think of the hearts you are breaking

        **G**                 **C**
And the pain you are bringing to me.


**(pg. 42/Side One, Sect. Four)**

## STREETS OF LAREDO

(I flat picked this one. Used the capo
on the second fret, and played it in
the key of C)

   C       G       C       G
*As I walked out in the streets of Laredo,*

   C       G       C       G
*As I walked out in Laredo one day*

   C       G       C       G
*I spied a poor cowboy a-wrapped in white linen,*

   C       F       G       C
*A-wrapped in white linen and cold as the clay.*


   C       G       C       G
*It's once in the saddle I used to go dashing*

   C       G       C       G
*It's once in the saddle I used to go gay*

   C       G       C       G
*First I turned to drinkin' and then to card playin'*

   C.      F       G       C
*I'm shot in the heart and I'm dying today.*


   C    G        C       G
*Let six jolly cowboys come carry my coffin*

   C       G       C       G
*And six pretty ladies to carry my pall*

   C       G       C       G
*Throw bunches of roses all over my coffin*

   C       F       G       C
*Throw roses to quiet the earth as it falls*


   C       G       C       G
*O beat the drum slowly and play the fife lowly*

   C       G       C       G
*Play the death march as we walk along*

   C       G       C       G
*Take me to the valley and lay the earth o'er me*

   C       F       G       C
*For I'm a poor cowboy and I know I've done wrong.*


**(pg. 43/Side One, Sect. Four)**

# I RIDE AN OLD PAINT

(I used a capo on the second fret for
 this one and flat picked it)

    **D**
I ride an old paint, I lead an old Dan,

  **A**               **D**
I'm goin' to Montana to throw a Hoolian

  **A**                  **D**
They feed 'em in the coolies, they water in the draw

  **A**             **D**
Their tails are all matted, their backs are all raw

  **A**             **D**
Ride around little dogies, ride around them slow

    **A**           **D**
For the fiery and the snuffy are rarin' to go


    **D**
When I die take my saddle from off the wall

  **A**             **D**
Put 'em on to my pony, lead him out of the stall

  **A**             **D**
Tie my bones to his back, turn our faces to the west

 **A**           **D**
Ride to the prairie that we love the best

  **A**             **D**
Ride around little dogies, ride around them slow

    **A**           **D**
For the fiery and the snuffy are rarin' to go


**(pg. 44/Side One, Sect. Four)**

## COLUMBUS STOCKADE

(Here's an extra Bluegrass song that we didn't learn earlier in this book, but it's on Side Four of your tapes, so you can hear it and learn the tune. I flat picked it and played it in the key of A)

   **A**                    **E**                            **A**
Way down in Columbus, Georgia, want to be back in Tennessee

   **A**                         **E**                                    **A**
Way down in Columbus Stockade, my friends all turned their backs on me

**D**                   **A**      **D**                **E**
Go and leave me if you wish to, never let is cross your mind

    **A**                   **E**                     **A**
If in your heart you love another, leave me little darlin' I don't mind


      **A**                  **E**                      **A**
Don't that road look rough and rocky, don't that sea look wide and deep

                         **E**                   **A**
Don't my darlin' look much sweeter, when he's in my arms asleep

**D**                   **A**      **D**                **E**
Go and leave me if you wish to, never let it cross your mind

    **A**                   **E**                     **A**
If in your heart you love another, leave me little darlin' I don't mind.

## THIS LITTLE LIGHT OF MINE
(I used a flat pick on this one)

**D**
This little light of mine, I'm gonna let it shine
**G**                            **D**
This little light of mine, I'm gonna let it shine

This little light of mine, I'm gonna let it shine
                 **A**       **D**     **G**
Every day, every day, every day, every day
     **A**        **D**
Gonna let my little light shine


**D**
Monday He gave me the gift of love,
**G**
Tuesday peace came from above,
**D**
Wednesday He told me to have more faith,
    **E**           **A**
On Thursday He gave me a little more grace
  **D**
On Friday, told me to watch and pray
**G**
Saturday told me just what to say
**D**                 **Bm**
Sunday He gave me the power Divine
   **E**   **A**    **D**
Just to let my little light shine (Chorus)

**(pg. 47/Side Two, Sect. One)**

## STEWBALL

**D**                                **Em**
*Stewball was a good horse, he wore a high head*

               **A**                         **D G A**
*And the mane on his foretop was as fine as silk thread*

              **D**                 **Em**
*I rode him in England, I rode him in Spain*

           **A**                 **D G A**
*And I never did lose boys, I always did gain*

            **D**               **Em**
*So come all you gamblers wherever you are*

           **A**               **D G A**
*And don't bet your money on the little grey mare*

           **D**             **Em**
*Most likely she'll stumble, most likely she'll fall*

        **A**               **D G A**
*But you never will lose boys on my noble Stewball*

           **D**             **Em**
*As they were a-riding 'bout halfway around*

           **A**             **D G A**
*That grey mare she stumbled and fell on the ground*

           **D**             **Em**
*Then away out yonder ahead of them all*

        **A**             **D G D**
*Came a-prancin' and a-dancin', my noble Stewball*

**(pg. 49/Side Two, Sect. One)**

## DOWN IN THE VALLEY

(I used a flat pick for this one and
changed some of the chords in the choruses)

C                               G
Down in the valley, the valley so low

                          C   G
Hang your head over, hear the wind blow

            C  Em* Am C†           Dm G
Hear the wind blow dear,     hear the wind blow

        Dm G          C  G
Hang your head over,   hear the wind blow


         C                 G
Roses love sunshine, violets love dew

                      C  G
Angels in heaven know I love you

          C     Em* Am C†      Dm G
Know I love you, dear,     know I love you

                      C
Angels in heaven know I love you

*play 5th string bass       †play 6th string bass

**(pg. 50/Side Two, Sect. Two)**


## MY HOME'S ACROSS THE BLUE RIDGE MOUNTAINS

   C
My home's across the Blue Ridge Mountains

  G                          C
My home's across the Blue Ridge Mountains

My home's across the Blue Ridge Mountains my love

  G                    C
And I never expect to see you anymore

  G                C
I never expect to see you anymore


  C
Goodbye honey, sugar, darlin',

  G              C
Goodbye honey, sugar, darlin',

*Goodbye honey, sugar, darlin',*
     **G**                        **C**
*And I never expect to see you anymore.*

**(pg. 51 / Side Two, Sect. Two)**

## KUMBAYA
(I used a capo at the second fret)

       **G**          **C**    **G**
*Kum Ba Ya, my Lord, Kum Ba Ya*
      **Bm**                 **D**
*Kum Ba Ya, my Lord, Kum Ba Ya*
       **G**        **C**     **G C G**   **D**    **G**
*Kum Ba Ya, my Lord, Kum Ba Ya, O Lord, Kum Ba Ya.*

         **G**          **C**   **G**
*Someone's singin', Lord, Kum Ba Ya*
        **Bm**              **D**
*Someone's singin', Lord, Kum Ba Ya*
         **G**       **C**     **G C G**   **D**    **G**
*Someone's singin', Lord, Kum Ba Ya, O Lord, Kum Ba Ya.*

       **G**          **C**    **G**
*Kum Ba Ya, my Lord, Kum Ba Ya*
      **Bm**                 **D**
*Kum Ba Ya, my Lord, Kum Ba Ya*
       **G**       **C**     **G C G**   **D**    **G**
*Kum Ba Ya, my Lord, Kum Ba Ya, O Lord, Kum Ba Ya.*

**(pg. 51 / Side Two, Sect. Three)**

## SHADY GROVE
(I used a capo at the second fret)

  **Am**           **G**         **Am**            **C**
*Cheeks as red as a bloomin' rose, eyes of the deepest brown*

  **Am**         **G**                 **Am**
*You are the darlin' of my heart, stay till the sun goes down*


  **Am**         **G**         **Am**        **C**
*Shady Grove, my little love, Shady Grove my dear*

  **Am**         **G**               **Am**
*Shady Grove, my little love, I'm gonna to leave you here*


  **Am**         **G**             **C**
*Shady Grove, my little love, standin' in the door*

  **Am**         **G**             **Am**
*Shoes and stockings in her hand, little bare feet on the floor*


  **Am**         **G**         **Am**      **C**
*Wished I had a big fine horse, corn to feed him on*

  **Am**         **G**             **Am**
*Pretty little girl to stay at home, feed him when I'm gone*


  **Am**         **G**         **Am**      **C**
*Shady Grove, my little love, Shady Grove my dear*

  **Am**         **G**             **Am**
*Shady Grove, my little love, I'm gonna to leave you here*

**(pg. 53/Side Two, Sect. Three)**


## SCARBOROUGH FAIRE

  **Am**         **G**         **Am**      **C**      **D**      **Am**
*Are you goin' to Scarborough Faire, parsley, sage, rosemary and thyme*

             **C**          **G**   **Am**   **G**      **Am**
*Remember me to one who lives there, she once was a true love of mine.*


  **Am**            **G**      **Am**      **C**      **D**      **Am**
*Tell her to make me a cambric shirt, parsley, sage, rosemary and thyme*

             **C**          **G**   **Am**   **G**      **Am**
*Without no seams or needlework, then she'll be a true love of mine*

<pre>
 Am              G    Am        C         D        Am
Tell her to find me an acre of land, parsley, sage, rosemary and thyme
            C               G    Am   G          Am
Between the salt water and the sea strand, then she'll be a true love of mine

 Am              G      Am        C         D        Am
Tell her to reap it with a sickle of leather, parsley, sage, rosemary and thyme
          C         G    Am   G          Am
And gather it all in a bunch of heather, then she'll be a true love of mine.
</pre>

**(pg. 53/Side Two, Sect. Three)**

## ST. JAMES INFIRMARY

(I added some extra chords on the "Let her go . . . " verse)

<pre>
     Am7   E7    Am7 E7      Am7         E7
I went down to old Joe's barroom on the corner by the square
     Am7      E7    Am7          E7      Am7
The drinks were served as usual, and the usual crowd was there
     Am7   E7    Am7                     E7
On my left stood big Joe McKennedy, and his eyes were bloodshot red
     Am7      E7  Am7           Dm       E7      Am7
He looked at the gang around him, and these were the words he said

     Am7      E7      Am7           E7
I went down to the St. James Infirmary, I saw my baby there
         Am7              E7      Am7   Dm    E7     Am7
She was stretched out on a long white table, so sweet, so cold, so fair
         C       E7    Am7              Dm       E7
Let her go, let her go, God bless her, wherever she may be
         Am7       E7      Am7       Dm        E7    Am7
You may search this wide world over, never find a gamblin' fool like me

     Am7  E7     Am7                          E7
And when I die please bury me in my hightop Stetson hat
     Am7       E7          Am7
Put a twenty dollar gold piece on my watch chain,
                     E7   Am7
So the gang'll know I'm standin' pat
     Am7   E7     Am7                            E7
I want six crap shooters for my pall bearers, a chorus line to sing a song
     Am7   E7    Am7           Dm        E7 Am7
Put a jazz band on my hearse wagon to raise hell as we roll along
</pre>

**(pg. 55/Side Two, Sect. Three)**

## GYPSY ROVER

(I didn't put this one on side four of your tapes)

```
    D       A       D       A
The gypsy rover come over the hill,

    D           A       D  A
Down through the valleys so shady

    D           A       D           G
He whistled and he sang till the green wood rang

    D       G       D G D A
And he won the heart of a la----dy
```

CHORUS:
```
D   A       D       A
A-ri-do-da-di-do-da-day

D   A       D   A
A-ri-do-da-di-day-di

    D                   D       G
He whistled and he sang till the green wood rang

    D       G       D G D
And he won the heart of a la----dy
```

```
    D       A           D   A   D           A       D A
Her father saddled his fastest steed, searched the valleys all o-ver

D           A   D   G           D       G   D G D A
Seeking his daughter at great speed and the whistling, gypsy ro----ver
```

```
    D       A           D   A   D       A   D A
At last he came to the river banks, upon the river Clayde

D           A       D       G           D   G   D G D A
There was music and there was wine for the gypsy and his la----dy
```

```
    D   A       D       A       D   A           D A
He is no gypsy, my father, she said, but lord of these lands all o-ver

    D   A       D   G           D       G   D G D A
And I will stay till my dying day with the whistling gypsy ro----ver
```

CHORUS

**(pg. 59/Side Two, Sect. Four)**

108

# WOKE UP THIS MORNING WITH MY MIND STAYED ON FREEDOM

**D**
*Woke up this morning with my mind stayed on freedom*
**G**                                                                      **D**
*Woke up this morning with my mind stayed on freedom*

*Woke up this morning with my mind stayed on freedom*
         **A**     **G D**
*Hallelu, Hallelu, Hallelu—ia*
**D**
*Ain't no harm to keep your mind stayed on freedom*
**G**                                                                      **D**
*Ain't no harm to keep your mind stayed on freedom*

*Ain't no harm to keep your mind stayed on freedom*
         **A**     **G D**
*Hallelu, Hallelu, Hallelu—ia*
**D**
*Walkin' and talkin' with my mind stayed on freedom*
**G**                                                                      **D**
*Walkin' and talkin' with my mind stayed on freedom*

*Walkin' and talkin' with my mind stayed on freedom*
         **A**     **G D**
*Hallelu, Hallelu, Hallelu—ia*

## SWING LOW, SWEET CHARIOT

```
C              F  C Am                    G
```
*Swing low, sweet chariot, comin' for to carry me home*
```
        C      F  C Am        G        C
```
*Swing low, sweet chariot, comin' for to carry me home*

```
   C                      F      C Am              G
```
*I looked over yonder and what did I see, comin' for to carry me home*
```
   C              F         C Am       G      C
```
*A band of angels comin' after me, comin' for to carry me home*

*CHORUS*

```
    C              F   C Am                G
```
*If you get there before I do, comin' for to carry me home*
```
    C              F       C Am       G        C
```
*Tell all my friends I'm comin' there too, comin' for to carry me home*

*CHORUS*

**(pg. 61/Side Two, Sect. Four)**

## WABASH CANNONBALL

(I used a capo on the first fret)
```
C                                              F
```
*Out from the wide Pacific to the broad Atlantic shore*
```
   G                                          C
```
*She climbs the flowery mountains over hills and by the shore*
```
                                                  F
```
*Although she's tall and handsome, she's known quite well by all*
```
   G                              C
```
*She's a regular combination, the Wabash Cannonball*

```
C                              F
```
*Listen to the jingle, the rumble and the roar*
```
   G                                          C
```
*As she glides along the woodlands over hills and by the shore*
```
   C                                          F
```
*She climbs the flowery mountains, hear the merry hobo squall*

     **G**                                      **C**
*As she glides along the woodland, the Wabash Cannonball*

    **C**                                         **F**
*Now the eastern states are dandy so the western people say*
    **G**                          **C**
*From New York to St. Louis, Chicago by the way*

                                        **F**
*Through the hills of Minnesota where the rippling waters fall*
    **G**                                **C**
*No chances to be taken on the Wabash Cannonball*

*CHORUS*

**(pg. 61/Side Three, Sect. One)**


## WAYFARING STRANGER
(I used a capo on the first fret and the full fingerpicking pattern)

    **Am E7**       **Am**           **Dm**           **Am E7**
*I am a poor   wayfaring stranger travelin' through this world of woe*
    **Am E**         **Am**           **Dm**        **Am**
*There's no sick - ness, toil or danger in that bright land to which I go*
    **F**           **C**         **F**        **E7**
*I'm goin' there to meet my mother, I'm goin' there no more to roam*
    **Am E**   **Am**         **Dm**     **Am**
*I'm just a-goin'  over Jordan, I'm just a-goin' over home.*

    **Am E7**        **Am**           **Dm**           **Am E7**
*I want to wear  the crown of glory, When I get home to that bright land*
    **Am E7**        **Am**        **Dm**      **Am**
*I want to shout  salvation's story together with the angel band*

*CHORUS*

**(pg. 63/Side Three, Sect. One)**

## GOOD SHEPHERD
*(I used a capo at the 1st fret.)*

    A  Am/3       Am/5  Am/3 A   Am/3        Am/5  Am/3
*If you want    to get to heaven,          over on the other shore*
A       Am/3     Am/5     Am/3
*Keep out of the way of the blood stained banner*
A     Am/3     E     A     Am/3 Am/5 Am/3
*Oh, Good Shepherd, feed my sheep.*
*Chorus:*
A    Am/3 Am/5  D    A     G       D     E
*One for Paul, one for Silas, one for to make my heart rejoice.*
A      Am/3     Am/5   D
*Can't you hear my lambs a-cryin',*
A     Am/3     E     A     Am/3 Am/5 Am/3
*Oh, Good Shepherd, feed my sheep.*
A      Am/3        Am/5  Am/3 A Am/3        Am/5  Am/3
*If you want to    make a heaven,       right where we are*
A       Am/3     Am/5     Am/3
*Keep out of the way of the long tongue liar*
A     Am/3     E     A     Am/3 Am/5 Am/3
*Oh, Good Shepherd, feed my sheep*
*Chorus*


## ONE MORNING IN MAY

    G         F          C        G
*One morning, one morning, one morning in May*
        F     C      D
*I spied a fair couple a-makin' their way*
G     Em     Am     G
*One was a maiden so bright and so fair*
            C        D     G
*And the other was a soldier and a brave volunteer*
    G         F        C       G
*Good morning, good morning, good morning, said he*
        F     C      D
*And where are you going my pretty lady*
    G     Em       Am     G
*I'm goin' out a-walkin' by, the banks of the sea*

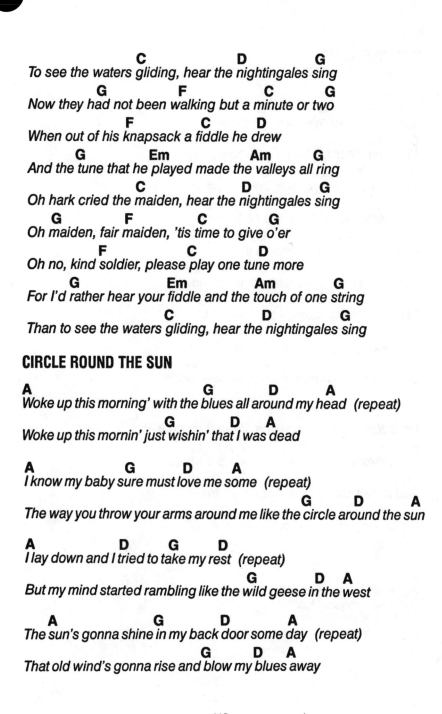

            **C**                **D**          **G**
*To see the waters gliding, hear the nightingales sing*

       **G**           **F**             **C**      **G**
*Now they had not been walking but a minute or two*

           **F**        **C**     **D**
*When out of his knapsack a fiddle he drew*

      **G**       **Em**        **Am**    **G**
*And the tune that he played made the valleys all ring*

            **C**          **D**         **G**
*Oh hark cried the maiden, hear the nightingales sing*

      **G**        **F**        **C**     **G**
*Oh maiden, fair maiden, 'tis time to give o'er*

           **F**        **C**     **D**
*Oh no, kind soldier, please play one tune more*

      **G**       **Em**        **Am**      **G**
*For I'd rather hear your fiddle and the touch of one string*

           **C**          **D**        **G**
*Than to see the waters gliding, hear the nightingales sing*

## CIRCLE ROUND THE SUN

**A**                       **G**        **D**    **A**
*Woke up this morning' with the blues all around my head  (repeat)*

                   **G**     **D**  **A**
*Woke up this mornin' just wishin' that I was dead*

**A**          **G**       **D**    **A**
*I know my baby sure must love me some  (repeat)*

                               **G**     **D**     **A**
*The way you throw your arms around me like the circle around the sun*

**A**        **D**    **G**    **D**
*I lay down and I tried to take my rest  (repeat)*

                       **G**        **D**  **A**
*But my mind started rambling like the wild geese in the west*

  **A**           **G**       **D**       **A**
*The sun's gonna shine in my back door some day  (repeat)*

                   **G**     **D**  **A**
*That old wind's gonna rise and blow my blues away*

## BYE, BYE, LOVE

*(I used a capo at the 4th fret and flatpicked this one)*
*Chorus:*

```
C       G   C       G
```
*Bye, bye, love, bye, bye, happiness*
```
C   G                   D       G
```
*Hello loneliness, I think I'm a-gonna cry*
```
C       G   C       G
```
*Bye, bye, love, bye, bye, sweet caress*
```
C   G               D       G
```
*Hello emptiness, I feel like I could die*
```
            D       G
```
*Bye, bye, my love-a goodbye*
```
            D               G
```
*There goes my baby with someone new*
```
            D               G
```
*She sure looks happy, I sure am blue*
```
            C               D
```
*She was my baby till he stepped in*
```
                            G
```
*Goodbye to romance that might have been*
*Chorus:*
```
            D                       G
```
*I'm-a through with romance, I'm-a through with love*
```
            D           G
```
*I'm-a through with countin' the stars above*
```
            C               D
```
*And here's the reason that I'm so free*
```
                            G
```
*My loving' baby is through with me*
*Chorus*

Words and music by B. and F. Bryant
© House of Bryant Music
All rights reserved.
Used by permission.

## GET ALONG LITTLE DOGIES
*(I flatpick this one and use a capo at the 1st fret.)*

   G      **Am**        D           D
As I was out walking one morning for pleasure
           **C**         D     G
I spied a cowpuncher a-riding along
   G          **Am**        D        G
His hat was thrown back and his spurs were a-jinglin'
          **C**       D      G
As he approached he was singing this song.
*Chorus:*

        D           **C**          G
Whoopie, ti yi yay, get along, little dogies
   D              **C**       G
It's your misfortune and none    of my own
          **Am**     D      G
Whoopie, ti yi yay, get along, little dogies
   **Em**     **Am**     D      G
You know that Wyoming will be your new home.
G      **Am**         D        G
Early in the springtime we'll round up the dogies
G      **C**      D       G
Slap on their brands and bob off their tails
         **Am**     D         G
Round up our horses, load up the chuckwagon
          **C**    D     G
Throw those dogies up on the trail
*Chorus*

         G        **Am**        D           G
When the night comes round and we hold 'em on the bed ground
      **C**      D   G
These little dogies that roll on so slow
     **Am**     D      G
Roll up the herd and cut out the strays
**C**      **C**      D       G
Roll the little dogies that never rolled before
*Chorus*

# HELP!
*(I used a capo at the 2nd fret .)*

**G**                           **Bm**
*When I was younger, so much younger than today*
**Em**                 **C**     **F**   **G**
*I never needed anybody's help in any way*
                                **Bm**
*But now those days are gone and I'm not so self assured*
**Em**                 **C**     **F**   **G**
*Now I find I've changed my mind, I've opened up the doors*
*Chorus:*
**Am**                      **F**
*Help me if you can I'm feelin' down, and I do appreciate you being 'round*
**D**                   **G**   **C**     **G**
*Help me get my feet back on the ground, won't you please, please help me*
**G**                     **Bm**
*And now my life has changed in oh so many ways*
**Em**                 **C**     **F**   **G**
*My independence seems to vanish in the haze*
**Bm**                 **Bm**
*But every now and then I feel so insecure*
**Em**                 **C**     **F**   **G**
*I know that I just need you like I've never done before*
*Chorus*

Words and music by John Lennon and
Paul McCartney

# Free Catalogue Request Form

*F*illed with juggling equipment, kites, harmonicas and instructional cassettes, as well as the entire library of Klutz books, the Flying Apparatus Catalogue has got to be the only one of its kind, anywhere. It's available free for the asking.

## So send me a catalog . . . .

*. . . And send my friend one too. He has this tiny little address.*

NAME _____

STREET _____

CITY/STATE _____

ZIP _____

NAME _____

STREET _____

CITY/STATE _____

ZIP _____

**K L U T Z / B O X  2 9 9 2 / S T A N F O R D ,  C A  9 4 3 0 5**

FLYING APPARATUS CATALOGUE

THE KLUTZ PRESS

### *Country & Blues Harmonica for the Musically Hopeless*

Jon Gindick is a harmonica instructor who doesn't believe in musical talent. ("I can't afford to. What if I don't have any?") His instructional book + cassette + Hohner harmonica has been a best-seller for us since its introduction in 1984. It's a musical first-aid kit that can bring out the rhythm in anybody.

**$12.95**

### The Banana Guitar Tuner

Small, handy and tone-deaf simple, electronic guitar tuners have leapt into mass usage over the past couple of years. All you do is pluck the string, and the needle tells you if you're sharp, flat or right on. Banana makes the basic no-frills model which we offer here at a discount. You'll need a 9-volt battery for it.

**$27.50**

## More Music from Carol McComb

When she's not teaching, Carol is an accomplished performer with three albums to her credit, one solo and two as part of the Gryphon Quintet. If you'd like to hear Carol sing and play, without stopping to tell you which chord she's on, you can order any or all of them right now.

**$8.95**

## Carol's Christmas Carols

A small, beautifully designed book with 12 classic Christmas carols arranged specifically for folk guitar by Carol McComb. Everyone knows the words, and the chord progressions are simple even by Hopeless standards. We're proud to offer it here. **$7.00**

## The Folksingers Wordbook

The basic resource. One thousand folk songs from every category: jugband, ragtime, ballads, calypso, rock and roll . . . just about everything. Includes words and chords. Compiled by Fred & Irwin Silberman.

**$17.50**

KLUTZ / BOX 2992 / STANFORD, CA 94305

# ORDERING BLANKS

| | QTY. | AMT. |
|---|---|---|
| Carol McComb's solo album, *LOVE CAN TAKE YOU HOME AGAIN:* **$8.95** | | |
| The Gryphon Quintet's first album: *THEY ALL LAUGHED* **$8.95** | | |
| The Gryphon Quintet's second album: *UNDECIDED* **$8.95** | | |
| *A GARLAND OF CHRISTMAS SONGS FOR FOLK GUITAR* **$7.00** by Carol McComb | | |
| *THE FOLKSINGERS WORDBOOK* **$17.50** | | |
| *COUNTRY AND BLUES HARMONICA FOR THE MUSICALLY HOPELESS* **$12.95** by Jon Gindick (book + cassette + Hohner harmonica) | | |
| Banana Guitar Tuner **$27.50** | | |
| *COUNTRY AND BLUES FOR THE MUSICALLY HOPELESS* **$12.95** by Carol McComb (book + 2 casettes) | | |
| | Add $1.00 for postage | |
| **TOTAL ENCLOSED** | | |

(check or money order.

NAME _____

STREET _____

CITY/STATE _____

ZIP _____

**Mail to Klutz/Box 2992/Stanford, CA 94305**